The Age o

Books by Charles Kovacs

Teacher resources

Class 4 (age 9–10)
Norse Mythology

Classes 4 and 5 (age 9–11)
The Human Being and the Animal World

Classes 5 and 6 (age 10–12)
Ancient Greece
Botany

Class 6 (age 11–12)
Ancient Rome

Classes 6 and 7 (age 11–13)
Geology and Astronomy

Class 7 (age 12–13)
The Age of Discovery

Classes 7 and 8 (age 12–14)
Muscles and Bones

Class 8 (age 13–14)
The Age of Revolution

Class 11 (age 16–17)
Parsifal and the Search for the Grail

General interest

The Apocalypse in Rudolf Steiner's Lecture Series
Christianity and the Ancient Mysteries
The Michael Letters of Rudolf Steiner
The Spiritual Background to Christian Festivals

The Age of Discovery

Charles Kovacs

Floris
Books

Publisher's note

The Age of Discovery is based on extensive lesson notes that were originally written by Charles Kovacs in the 1960s, and reflect the author's understanding of history and his views on the subject. In this revised edition we have removed some chapters and updated some language to better reflect contemporary interpretations. We recommend reading this book with an understanding of the context in which it was written.

First published in volume form in 2004
This edition published 2023
© 2004 Estate of Charles Kovacs
The author has asserted his right under the Copyright, Design and Patents Act 1988 to be identified as the Author of this Work. All right reserved. No part of this publication may be reproduced without the prior permission of Floris Books, Edinburgh www.florisbooks.co.uk

 Also available as an eBook

British Library CIP Data available
ISBN 978-178250-851-9
Printed in Great Britain by
Bell & Bain Ltd

MIX
Paper | Supporting
responsible forestry
FSC® C007785

Printed on sustainably sourced FSC® certified paper. Uses plant-based inks which reduce chemical emissions.

Contents

Foreword

Foreword

Charles Kovacs was a teacher at the Rudolf Steiner School in Edinburgh for many years. During his time he wrote extensive notes of his lessons, day by day. Since then these texts have been used and appreciated by teachers in Edinburgh and other Steiner-Waldorf schools. This book represents the way one teacher taught a particular group of children. While some of the detail in this book may not be relevant in teaching history today in other countries, what is nevertheless interesting is how Kovacs picks out pertinent stories for the context in which he was teaching, and creates a tapestry showing the development of humankind from the Crusades, where Europeans discovered new ideas and a refined civilisation in the Arab world, to the awakening intellectual curiosity of the Renaissance, which led to the exploration of more parts of the world, new artistic and religious forms, as well as countless inventions.

This period of history is ideally suited for children around the age of thirteen, when in their own soul they experience a similar awakening and desire to widen their horizons and explore the world around them.

Astrid Maclean, Edinburgh 2004

1. The Crusades

Think how many times there have been invasions of Britain: the Romans, the Anglo-Saxons, the Danes, the Normans. Each one of these invaders has left their mark on the English language. For example, from Roman times comes the word 'master', from the Latin *magister*, meaning a superior person. From the Anglo-Saxons come nearly all words about farming: wheat, rye, oats, horse, cow, house. From the Danes come most of the words beginning with 'sk': sky, skin, skull, skill. From the Normans come French words like mutton (from *mouton*, sheep), pork (from *porc*, pig), and court. Our language is really a mixture of many languages, and this is also the reason for the difficult spelling, for it is also a mixture of different spellings. In Anglo-Saxon words 'ou' is pronounced as in 'house', but in Norman words the pronunciation is as in 'court'.

But there are also words in our language that come from a people who never invaded Britain, and these are the Arabs. We have Arabic words in our language such as alcohol, sugar and sofa. These words came into our language through the Crusades, and we shall look at how the Crusades began.

The Christian religion meant much to people in Western Europe. Poor farmers willingly gave one tenth (the tithe) of their crop to the monks; knights and kings made great gifts of land to monasteries and churches, and people spared no money or effort to build their churches as beautifully as they could. But this was not all. In every Christian land there were people who felt the most wonderful thing in life would be to see with their own eyes the place where Jesus Christ had walked: the Holy Land and Jerusalem, the Holy City. A person who had this great longing to see the Holy Land had to make a very long and arduous journey in those days. It took years before they saw their homeland again. Such a person was called a pilgrim, and the journey was called a pilgrimage. A pilgrim often wore special clothes that told everyone that this was a pilgrim who must be helped with food, shelter or money, for it was a Christian's duty to assist a pilgrim. The pilgrims wore a hat with shells on it and a garment that reached down to their ankles. They carried a little satchel, called a scrip, on a belt and a long staff with a cross on top. In those days, when people felt that their religion was the most important thing in life, there were always hundreds of people coming or going on that great journey.

The Arabs, who now controlled the Holy Land and Jerusalem, were Muslims, but they allowed these Christian pilgrims to come to Jerusalem, to say their prayers at the holy places and return again to their homelands. But around the time of the Battle of Hastings, when William the Conqueror and his Normans invaded England, something happened in the faraway lands of the East.

From the East, from Asia, came the Seljuk Turks, who had long ago embraced Islam, so they did not attack the Arab kingdom for religious reasons, but for reasons of conquest. When Jerusalem fell into their hands in 1071, the Seljuks stabled their horses in the places holy to Christians and no longer allowed pilgrims to come.

When news of this reached the Christians in Europe, it came as a terrible shock. In 1095, Pope Urban II called a great council in the city of Clermont in France. It was a mighty gathering. Lords and noblemen who commanded thousands of men, knights who had only a handful of vassals, kings and bishops, monks and peasants, people from every country. Pope Urban held a sermon and called upon them to take up arms and drive the Seljuks from the Holy Land.

'Consider, therefore,' he said, 'that the Almighty has created you for this purpose, that through you he may restore Jerusalem.'

And like a roar of thunder there came from all these thousands of men the cry: '*Dieu le volt* (God wills it).'* As a sign that they devoted their lives and all their possessions to the task of fighting for the Holy Land, they sewed red strips of cloth in

---

* In modern French '*Dieu le veut*'.

the form of a cross on their breast and shoulders. It was the sign of the War of the Cross, or the Crusade as they called it.

From the Council of Clermont the knights hastened home and prepared themselves for the long journey. Many of them sold their land and their castles in order to have money for the expedition. Not only knights, but also villagers and serfs who worked for the knights, left their ploughs to become Crusaders, and no master dared to hold them back. Merchants left their shops, shepherds their flocks, men with wives and children left their families to the care of God and set out. Monks went to every village to tell people about the Crusade. Because this call to arms was met with such an enthusiastic response from all levels of society, the first army to set out for the Holy Land in 1096 became known as the People's Crusade.

With everything done in such haste it was not surprising that this first army of Crusaders came to a sorry end. This first army of Crusaders consisted mainly of peasants who had no money to pay for their food. At first they marched through countries where the people gave them food, but when they came to Byzantium (now called Greece and the Balkans) the Byzantines (who did not recognise the authority of the Pope) would not give them any food without being paid for it. The Crusaders then took what they needed by force. The Byzantine Emperor provided ships to move the ragged army across the Bosporus to Asia Minor. There they were attacked by Seljuks.

After the first army of Crusaders was defeated, a much better prepared and well-organised army was gathered in France. This became known as the Prince's Crusade and was under the command of one of the bravest knights in Christendom: Godfrey de Bouillon.

2. Godfrey de Bouillon

Before we look further at the so-called Prince's Crusade, we must try to understand why hundreds of thousands of people in Britain and France, in Germany and Italy, were willing to leave their homes, their families and their possessions, to set out on a long and terrible journey that would bring them great hardship and, perhaps, death in battle.

How was it that hundreds of thousands of men from every walk of life – knights and villagers, merchants and tradesmen – willingly and joyfully, pinned the red Crusader's cross on their breasts and set out on a journey from which, as they knew, many would not return?

First, there was a feeling of anger that the most holy place for any Christian – the tomb where Christ had risen from the dead – should be in the hands of the people who desecrated it by stabling horses there, and who would not allow any Christian to come to Jerusalem. To them it was shameful to let such a thing happen, and they considered it a holy duty to wrest holy places from the grip of the Seljuk Turks. For most Crusaders this was the main reason. They believed that they were doing the will of God by joining the Crusade.

But for some Crusaders there were also other reasons. Let us take Fred, a villager. Fred certainly wanted to do the will of God and help take back the Holy Land from the Seljuks. But he also thought that by joining the Crusaders he could get away from the endless hard work he did for his master and lord. Perhaps he would even gain a knighthood for himself by brave deeds in battle. And who knew what riches could be taken from the enemy? In the Christian lands there was very little gold, but in the East there was a great deal of it. So for Fred, there was not only the holy duty of fighting the Seljuks, there was also the hope of freedom – that he might come back a knight, a free man, with a lot of gold. There were hundreds of thousands of villagers and serfs like Fred.

A knight like Godfrey de Bouillon, however, had no wish to enrich himself by going on a crusade. Yet for Godfrey, too, there was not only the holy duty to take back the Holy Land, there was also another reason. We could have heard this reason if we had been present at a meeting Godfrey had with his closest friends. At this meeting Godfrey said: 'We are all friends here and so I can speak freely without fear that what I say will be betrayed to monks and priests, and what I want to say is this: I am sure you all feel as I do that our Christian Church, which we love wholeheartedly, is not what it should be, for it is under the absolute authority of the Pope in Rome. No one is allowed to think for themselves, no one is allowed to ask questions about religion or the Church; if anyone does so, he is called a bad Christian and threatened with punishment. Kings and lords have to obey the wishes of the Pope in worldly matters as well as in religion. Surely, this is not what Christ wanted. But in the East, in Greece, in Constantinople there are Christians who do not recognise the Pope. Perhaps we can learn from them. Perhaps, when we have taken Jerusalem back from the Seljuks, we shall be able to make the Holy City the centre of a new Christian Church, a Church independent of Rome and independent of the Pope. My friends, let us hope that, in time, the new free Church of Jerusalem will take the place of the unfree Church of Rome where everyone is under authority of the Pope.'

This is what Godfrey said to his closest friends who all thought as he did. For them this hope of a new Church was another reason to join a Crusade. As we will see later on, this hope was not fulfilled, but it was in the hearts of some knights when they set out.

So among both villagers and knights there were all kinds of reasons to join the Crusades besides the religious fervour to take back the Holy Land.

Now Godfrey de Bouillon was in command of the second wave of Crusaders, a great army of a hundred thousand men, mainly French and German. The knights of this army had sold their land and castles to have money to pay for their journey. They marched through France, Germany, Hungary, through the Balkan peninsula and Greece, then they passed through Constantinople. Unfortunately, the Crusaders did not remain friendly with the Christian people of Constantinople. When they saw all the gold and wealth there many soldiers were driven to rob and plunder.

When the Crusaders came to Syria, the country north of the Holy Land, they had their first battles. But they also encountered other enemies more fearsome than the Turks. The worst of these enemies was the hot climate. The heavy, iron armour that the Crusaders wore became a ghastly burden in the scorching sun. On top of that, the Crusaders were not used to washing themselves properly, and soon infectious diseases broke out that killed thousands of Crusaders as they had no doctors to treat them.

For three years the Crusaders battled through Syria; they lost more men through epidemics than through fighting. When at long last they had fought their way to Palestine and came before Jerusalem, there were only twenty thousand Crusaders left – one hundred thousand had set out. But for these twenty thousand it was a great day. When they saw the Holy City of Jerusalem before them, knights and common soldiers cried out with joy, some sank to their knees and kissed the ground to thank God for being allowed to see the Holy City.

But Godfrey de Bouillon was deeply worried. He had only twenty thousand men and Jerusalem was not only surrounded by high, thick walls, but also defended by sixty thousand Turks. However, the Crusaders readied themselves to assault the city.

After five days of preparation the first assault was made. The Crusaders carried long rope-ladders with grappling-hooks. They threw the ladders high up and the hooks gripped the top of the wall, allowing the Crusaders to climb up. But the Seljuks knew how to deal with them. They cut the rope of the ladders with their swords and the Crusaders crashed to the ground. After a day in which they lost many men, the Crusaders returned to their camp, sadder but also wiser. They realised now that they had to build siege-towers to take the city. They set to work, knights working side by side with villagers and serfs as they cut down trees in a nearby forest. From the wood they built towers on wheels, towers as high as the walls.

And so, at long last, came the day of the assault. But before the assault was made something else took place. The whole Crusader army formed a great procession and, well out of reach of Seljuk arrows, they walked around the walls of Jerusalem, singing hymns and saying prayers. When they had completed the round, trumpets sounded and the assault began. The creaking towers with knights on the top were pushed to the walls. The Seljuks sent hails of arrows against the approaching towers. They also shot flaming arrows at the towers, and here and there these flaming arrows set a siege-tower on fire, but other towers reached the walls. The Seljuks poured buckets of boiling oil onto the Crusaders, but still they came.

Then the bridge of one tower touched the top of the wall, a knight rushed across – the first to set foot on the wall – it was Godfrey de Bouillon. A great shout: '*Dieu le volt*, God wills it,' rose from the Crusaders when they saw Godfrey defending his foothold against the Seljuks. Then another knight joined him and another. Now Crusaders from other towers gained the walls. After fierce fighting the Seljuks were driven from the walls, but now the battle continued in the streets of Jerusalem and the Crusaders fought for every house.

It is sad to say that in this furious battle inside the city, women and children too were killed by the Crusaders. When the fighting was over and Jerusalem was in the hands of the Crusaders, Godfrey, the commander, took off his armour and his weapons and, dressed only in the coarse long shirt of a pilgrim, he walked barefoot to the tomb where Christ rose from the dead, and remained there in silent prayer.[*]

The year Jerusalem was taken by the Crusaders was 1099. Most of those who had set out had died. Sometimes in old churches you find the tomb of a Crusader knight. On such tombs there is a carving of the knight with his arms crossed over

---

[*] To this day one can see the hundreds of crosses the Crusader knights carved in the wall of the church at the tomb.

his chest. If there is a lion under his feet it means that he died on a Crusade.

Now the Holy Land had become a new Christian country, and the Crusader knights offered Godfrey the crown of this new country, called the Kingdom of Jerusalem. But Godfrey was too modest, and he refused. And so his brother, Baldwin, became the first king of Jerusalem. This Kingdom lasted for eighty-eight years, and in that time Christian pilgrims could safely come and visit the holy places.

3. Saladin and Richard the Lionheart

The Crusaders' Kingdom, the Kingdom of Jerusalem, was also called the Frankish Kingdom, as most of the knights came from France. Many of the knights had sold their lands and their castles to have money for their long journey, and when the Crusade was finished they had no home to go back to. So many knights stayed and built castles for themselves. One can still see some of these Crusader castles there today.

Over time they saw how the Muslim Turks and Arabs lived, and they saw that there were many good things to learn from them. There was the use of sugar to make things sweet; in Europe people had only known honey. They found the sugar made from sugarcane much more useful for cooking. That was how the Arabic word *sukkar* and the use of sugar came to us. They also saw that the Turks and Arabs used many spices with their food: pepper, but also ginger, mustard, cinnamon and many others. But it was not only the knights in the Holy Land who came to like spices in their food. People in Europe had to eat meat that was kept in salt all through the winter to preserve it, which tasted and smelled horrible. But when they heard of spices, they added them too, and the salty taste and nasty smell disappeared. Soon many people in Europe wanted to eat heavily spiced food. And so a great trade in spices from the East began.

But in the long run, the Frankish knights could not keep the Holy Land. For about eighty-eight years, less than three generations, they held the land, but then there arose a Muslim leader who was not only a great general and warrior, but a man of noble character. This man's name was Saladin, and he united the Muslims of Egypt, Syria, Yemen and Palestine, and became their leader. Under Sultan Saladin, the Muslim army stormed into the Holy Land and reconquered Jerusalem. But Saladin was a generous man. None of the women or children in Jerusalem were harmed and they were allowed to leave Jerusalem and to go to Tyre in the north of the Holy Land, which was still held by Christian knights. Even the men who were taken prisoner were well treated and if their families paid a ransom for them, they were released. The Christian Crusaders had never treated the Muslims so generously.

The fall of Jerusalem in 1187 came as bitter news to the people in the Christian lands of Europe. Again, the call for a Crusade went out and three powerful rulers agreed to join forces and lead their armies against Saladin. One was the king of England, Richard the Lionheart, the other was Philip, king of France, and the third was Duke Leopold of Austria.

From the beginning, the pride and jealousy between these three rulers was so strong that they could not work together. They would not even attack an enemy fortress together. Instead it was arranged that their forces would attack on alternate days. In the end the fortress surrendered and Saladin paid a great ransom for the safe return of his soldiers. But Philip and Richard the Lionheart quarrelled so fiercely over the division of the gold, that the French king decided he had had enough of the Crusade and sailed home with his army.

Soon after that Richard the Lionheart had another quarrel with the duke of Austria. The Austrians had stormed the walls of another enemy fortress and raised their flag, but Richard came and tore it down. And so the Austrians, too, left Richard, swearing they would revenge the insult. The English now had to fight Saladin and his armies alone. But Richard the Lionheart, although he was proud and conceited, was a fearless leader and his knights loved him. There is a little story that shows how faithful the English knights were to their king as well as showing what a great and noble person Saladin was.

On one occasion Richard the Lionheart and a few knights left the camp of the English army and went hunting. The hunt took them further and further away until they were many miles from their soldiers. Suddenly a band of Saladin's horsemen appeared and attacked the group of hunters. The Crusaders fought valiantly, but they were outnumbered. Suddenly, one of the English knights called out: 'I am Richard, the King. Come and fight me, you cowards!' Immediately the horsemen threw ropes over him to bring this precious prisoner alive to Saladin. While they were busy with this prisoner, the real Richard and the other knights galloped away and escaped. The brave knight was brought before Saladin who immediately recognised that the prisoner was not King Richard. The knight told Saladin what he had done. Saladin praised him and sent a message saying that in exchange for ten Muslim prisoners the king could have his faithful knight back. Richard agreed gladly.

For a whole year the English Crusaders battled against Saladin. But despite their courage, this small army could not regain Jerusalem. They came so near that they could see the Holy City in the distance, but they could not come any closer, they could not defeat Saladin.

In that year of battles Richard and Saladin had learned not only to respect each other but even to think very highly of each other. And so they came together to make peace. Saladin, of course, would not give up Jerusalem, it remained in the hands of the Muslims, but he agreed that Christian pilgrims could come to Jerusalem unhindered and could worship in the holy places. That was all Richard could achieve, and more than he could hope for because Saladin might just as easily have kept the pilgrims out.

So Richard set out for England and for home. But his troubles were not yet over. The ship in which he sailed was wrecked in a storm and he barely escaped with his life. Disguised as a pilgrim he made his way through Greece, the Balkans and up the River Danube through Austria. But there he was recognised by a man who had been in the Crusade, and the duke of Austria had not forgotten the insult done to him. Richard the Lionheart was taken and imprisoned in a castle on the Danube.

His people in England had no news from him. They did not know whether he was alive or dead. But Richard had a faithful friend, a minstrel called Blondin who went to search for his king. He went from castle to castle singing a tune he and King

Richard had often sung together. After many months he came to Castle Dürnstein where Richard was kept, and when Blondin sang the first bars of the tune he heard a voice inside the castle sing the next bars. Now he knew where King Richard was. He hastened back to England and the English lords offered such a great ransom to the duke of Austria that he agreed to let Richard return.

4. The Changes in Europe

The Crusades started with enthusiasm. Noblemen sold their lands, fathers left their families, knights and villagers went willingly to give their life in order to rescue the Holy Land from the Muslims. But what happened later? After they had taken Jerusalem the Crusaders who had settled in the Holy Land lived more like the people in the East, and the Crusaders from Europe quarrelled so much amongst themselves that they could not defeat the Muslims.

In the end the Holy Land was retaken by the Muslims, and of the Crusaders' Kingdom, the Kingdom of Jerusalem, nothing remained except a few ruined castles. Although the Crusades were a terrible waste of human lives – a great effort and a great suffering – some good did eventually come from them. While the people in Europe had hoped in vain to gain the Holy Land, Europe gained a great deal in the end – it gained things no one had thought of when the Crusades started.

Before the Crusades, a peasant from France or from Britain had only ever seen his little piece of land in his homeland and the limited ways of farming of his father and grandfather. He had lived in a crude cottage and did not know that life could be different. But then this man 'took the Cross' and went east and saw how people lived there, and when he came back again he surprised the people of his village when he opened a little bag and showed a few seeds, saying: 'We and our fathers before us have never known any other wheat than one with short stalks and about six grains on each ear. But in the East I have seen wheat with proud long stalks and twenty grains or more on each ear. I have brought the seed grains with me. In a few years' time we shall all have three or four times more golden yield in our fields – three or four times more food for ourselves.'

He also said: 'Another thing I saw was that people in the East use cows' manure to keep their fields fertile. That's another thing to give us more and much better food. I have also brought seeds of plants you have never seen before: cabbage, carrots, spinach, cauliflower. And also fruit you have never heard of before: apricots, peaches, plums.'

The villagers could hardly believe him, but a few years later they saw his rich yield of corn, his tasty vegetables, his juicy fruit and asked the Crusader for the seeds of these wonderful plants. So the Crusades brought better ways of farming, as well as new food to Europe.

Another thing the Crusaders had never seen before was a beautiful flower-garden. They liked the gardens so much that they brought the seeds and the art of gardening back to Europe. Certain flowers – tulips, lilies and carnations – and the love of flowers, the knowledge of when to plant each kind, were brought to Europe by the Crusaders. They also brought home the art of making perfume from flowers. The words *sugar, candy* and *syrup* are Arab words, and the knowledge to make candy and syrup was brought to Europe by the Crusaders.

Before the Crusades, people in Europe knew no other seating than hard chairs or stools. But in the East they saw people recline comfortably on cushioned seats, called *sofas* and *divans* in Arabic. They also saw that the Arabs did not sleep on the wooden planks of a bed, but put something they called a *mattress* on the boards. These words as well as these objects came to Europe through the Crusades.

The story of paper is also interesting. It was the Chinese who first invented a way to use sawdust and old rags, adding water and acid to make a soggy mess called 'pulp', which they then spread in thin layers on a board. When it dried it became a sheet of paper. The Chinese were the first to have paper. The Arabs, in one of their expeditions to the Far East, captured some Chinese people and from them they learned how to make paper. The Crusaders learnt it from the Arabs and brought the knowledge to Europe.

But it was a smith in the city of Damascus who discovered that if you take an iron sword, heat it until it is red hot, and then plunge it into cold water, the iron becomes not only harder but also more flexible – it becomes steel. The making of steel was another thing brought back by the Crusaders.

To their surprise, the Crusaders saw Turkish and Arab sailors on their sea journeys use a little piece of magnetic iron which always pointed north – a compass. But this too was originally a Chinese invention. From the Turks the Crusaders learned the use of drums for marching; they found it was much easier to march to the steady beat of the drum.

In the workshops of the East the Crusaders also saw incredible leather work, beautifully carved and varnished furniture, and cloth dyed in many colours. All this was unknown in Europe and now became known through the Crusaders. New crafts grew up in Europe, and soon the people there could make things that the Arabs and Turks liked and were willing to pay for. And so, through trade, money began to come back to Europe.

Through the Crusades great improvements came about in all people's lives: food, flowers, comforts. But there was also something else – a great change in people's minds. The people who went on the first Crusades considered anyone who was not a Christian like themselves to be an evil person. They could not imagine that anyone who was not a Christian by religion could be kind, generous or in any way a good person. And because they had this idea in their heads they were merciless in their battles. But then they came to know such people as Sultan Saladin, a man who was not a Christian but who had more fairness, nobility and courage than many a Christian knight. Even Richard the Lionheart – who did not respect other people easily – felt a deep respect and admiration for Saladin. People in Europe began to realise that a person is good through their heart, not because they are a Christian or a Jew or a Muslim, and that one must respect a person for what they are in themselves and not judge them by their religion.

In the East, the Crusaders also met people who were Christians but did not recognise the authority of the Pope, like the people of Constantinople. Some of them began to wonder if there could be a Church that was not ruled over by the Pope in Rome.

Not only material things, but also *ideas* were exchanged through the Crusades. The Arabs' knowledge of science, like astronomy or medicine, stirred the minds of the Europeans. The people of Europe had not gained the Holy Land, but they had become more awake, more open to the world. This was the real gain of the Crusades.

Europe had become richer in material things as well as in ideas. Without the Crusades the Christian peoples of Europe might have carried on in their simple ways without even knowing that life could be different.

5. The Growth of Cities

Although the Crusades ultimately failed to take control of the Holy Land, Europe nevertheless gained new knowledge from the cultural exchange that resulted. The pilgrims and the Crusaders brought back better grain, new plants to eat (cabbage, cauliflower), new fruit (apricots), new crafts (glassmaking, leather work), better ways of building, and many other changes. But the most important of all the changes that came with the Crusades was the growth of cities.

Roman life had been concentrated in cities, but when the Germanic tribes destroyed the Roman Empire they also destroyed the cities. The Germanic tribes did not like to be crowded together, they preferred the free, open countryside, and so many cities declined or disappeared. People lived in villages, huddling under the protection of a castle, and few people ventured far from their home.

But when the Crusades came, the little fishermen's village of Venice on the coast of Italy, for example, suddenly grew. Crusaders and pilgrims wanted to go by sea to the Holy Land and paid the fishermen to take them over in their boats. These fares paid by thousands of travellers made the fishermen rich. Venice grew into a city of wealthy merchants. And when the people of Europe grew fond of spices in their food, it was again the merchants of Venice who carried the spices from the East to Europe and made huge profits. Venice became richer and grew larger, it could afford its own army of mercenaries who were paid to fight for Venice. It had become a powerful city built on business and trade.

Similar things happened all over Europe. Pilgrims and Crusaders travelled on rivers, which were quicker and safer than the poor roads of that time, and where these travellers stopped for a rest or for food, cities began to grow.

Business and trade were what made new cities rise in Europe. But there was something else. Before the Crusades, villagers and serfs were hardly better off than slaves, but a villager or serf who came back from the Crusades had seen the world. He had perhaps learned a new craft and had no wish to go back to a life of serfdom to a knight. A serf could do two things to gain freedom: he could buy his freedom by paying his master a sum of money (but not many serfs had enough to buy their freedom), or he could simply run away. Just running away was not much use, for fleeing from one's lord was a crime punishable by death. But there was a special law for the new cities: if a serf or a villager ran away from his lord and came into a city, and if he lived in the city without being caught for a year and a day, he was free. His master could neither claim him nor punish him. The serf had become a free man.

A good many serfs and villagers escaped to the new cities to live as free men. In a city, no one could 'own' a fellow man – every member of the city was a free person, a citizen or burgher, and very proud of it. The free citizens chose or elected their own city government, the town council. No knight, no lord, could rule them, and even knights had to respect the freedom of the cities.

The cities became places where freedom could grow while the castles and villages were still places of serfdom. So the Crusades started business and trade in the cities, and as the cities grew they also became the birth place of a new freedom in Europe.

What did a medieval city look like?

Approaching from a distance we would see a great wall surrounding the city. On the wall were watchtowers, and there were gates and drawbridges over the moat below the wall. Every city was like a fortress, ready to defend itself. All citizens were trained in the use of arms, especially in the use of the crossbow, which was also an invention that had come from the East.

In the centre of the city there was a high tower, called the belfry. High up in this tower there was always a watchman on duty ready to ring a great bell if he saw any armed force appear.

Passing through one of the gates into the city, we would immediately have realised that the great wall that protected the city also had disadvantages. Once the wall was built, the city could no longer grow and spread; new people came, new houses were built, but all in the space inside the walls. And so a medieval city was terribly crammed and crowded: the houses were huddled together, the streets were incredibly narrow – barely wide enough for an ox-cart – and they twisted and turned in every direction.

But the worst thing about these winding streets was that everyone treated them as rubbish-heaps. There was no sanitation or lavatories in the houses. Buckets full of refuse were emptied through the windows into the street below, and if a dog or a cat died it was also thrown out into the street. In and out of this rubbish and dirt walked pigs and chickens and rats looking for food.

At night there was no street lighting. At nine o'clock the curfew bell tolled from a tower. Curfew comes from *couvre feu*, which is French for 'cover the fire', and when this bell tolled all lights – all candles and burning torches for there were no other lights – had to be extinguished. This was to prevent fires at night. In the dark, the nightwatchmen patrolled the streets to prevent burglary and theft, and every hour they sang the time.

There was only one large open space in the city, the marketplace. On a weekday morning the peasants from the surrounding countryside came in to sell milk, butter and vegetables. In the marketplace you might see an important-looking man swinging a hand-bell – this was the town-crier. When a crowd of people had been called together by his bell, he told them the important news or proclamations from the town council. Today we have media like newspapers, radio and television. In those days the town-crier was all these rolled into one.

In another corner of the marketplace there were the stocks and the pillory, to punish butchers, bakers or other tradesmen who cheated their customers. They had to sit or stand in these wooden frameworks which had holes for the head and limbs, and their fellow citizens could heap abuse and scorn on them.

As in the East, all shops of the same trade were in the same street: cobbler's lane, tailor's street, and so on. These shops had only picture signs – a shoe, a pair of scissors, a barber's pole – because most people could not read.

You might think there was no beauty in such a city of the Middle Ages. But there was. Coming out of a narrow lane you might see a great church with high, lofty spires. These churches had stained-glass windows and from the inside they glowed in wonderful colours as the light shone through them. The pointed arches above were like hands in prayer. This style of building is known as Gothic, and it was a style that the Crusaders brought back from the East.

These stained-glass windows were so big that there was very little wall left between them, and it seemed a wonder how such narrow wedges of wall could support the high vaults and the great tower above them. But the vaults and the tower were supported by rows of strong pillars inside the church and by flying buttresses outside. Inside and outside the Gothic church had stone and wood carvings showing stories from the Old and New Testament of the Bible.

Before the Crusades, Europe had been poor, without freedom and with little art. Now, within the Gothic churches, art and beauty came back. The cities of the Middle Ages were crowded and unsanitary compared with our cities today, but they were the cradle of freedom and art, and of a new civilisation in Europe.

6. King John and the Magna Carta

The cities where all citizens were equal were the cradles of freedom in Europe. Under the old feudal system there were serfs, above them villagers, above them knights and above them the king. In this feudal system everyone (except the king) had an overlord who had to be obeyed. But with the cities something new came about: men of the city only obeyed the town council, which they themselves had elected. The citizens did not belong to the feudal system.

At first it was only the city people, the burghers, who had this kind of freedom, but in time the whole feudal system came to an end. One of the most important changes in British history came in the year 1215.

Richard the Lionheart, the valiant Crusader, was away from England for many years, first on his Crusade, then as a prisoner in Austria. He could only give a very little time to the task of ruling England. When he returned he did not live long and he died without leaving any children. Now Richard had two brothers. Geoffrey had died before Richard and so his son, Arthur, was to inherit the throne. But Arthur was only a young boy, and so Richard's other brother, John, became king.

King John was as wicked and evil a man as ever ruled a country. The story of his misdeeds and cruelty would fill books. One of his first misdeeds was against his nephew, the boy Arthur. John wanted him out of the way so that when Arthur grew up he could not claim the throne.

When William the Conqueror had conquered England, he remained master of Normandy on the other side of the Channel, and the kings who followed him also ruled Normandy as well as England. The north of France was at that time under the rule of the kings of England.

King John sent his little nephew to a lonely castle in Normandy where he was kept prisoner. One day King John came to visit the castle and spent the night there. We shall never know what happened that night, but the little Prince Arthur was never seen again.

Having made sure that there was no competitor for the throne, John now showed his noblemen, the knights of England, that, as their overlord, he stood above the law. He could do as he liked.

One of the English noblemen was engaged to a very beautiful lady. King John saw her, and decided he wanted her for himself. So he sent armed men to kidnap her when she went for a walk and then she was held captive in a castle until, in the end, she agreed to marry King John.

And so it was in many other things. King John showed that no one had any rights in his land: not his noblemen, not the priests, not the common people. He took what he wanted and used his soldiers against anybody who resisted. This brother of the noble Richard the Lionheart became one of the worst tyrants in British history.

By this time, people were no longer willing to put up with such treatment. A number of English lords and noblemen met secretly and swore an oath that they would help each other to force this wicked king to respect the rights of his people.

They made a list of all the things a king should not be allowed to do, and they wrote down the rights that everyone in the land should have and which no one could take from them. A list was called a charter in those days, and this long list was called the Great Charter or, in Latin, *Magna Carta*.

The Magna Carta, the great list of rights, is one of the most famous documents in history. One of the original copies is in the British Library in London. Today we take it for granted that the king or queen or the government cannot simply come and take our property away. We take it for granted that no person can be thrown into prison just because some powerful person does not like them. But all this was quite possible until these English knights wrote in the Magna Carta that it should not be allowed. That is why the Magna Carta is so important. For the first time the peoples of a country laid down rules for their kings and wrote down their rights, which no king could take from them.

When the knights had made this list, the Magna Carta, they took it to King John and asked that he should sign it with his name, to show that he would from now on respect the rules set out in it. But King John refused – no one was to have any rights but the king himself.

Now it was not always the case that the people of England were united amongst themselves. The common people were pleased when the noblemen were in trouble. The knights and noblemen often had quarrels and fights with the cities, and the priests often sided with the king. But this time priests, knights, peasants and citizens were all united against King John.

A great army was assembled and marched towards London to force King John to put his name to the Magna Carta. When King John tried to get his army together, he found that, in the whole of England, only seven knights were ready to fight for him.

So King John could do nothing but meet the rebels. This meeting took place at Runnymede, near London, in the year 1215.

Once again the noblemen put the Magna Carta before King John for his signature. King John cursed and swore, he shouted: 'Why don't you ask me to give my whole kingdom away?' But when he looked at the stern faces around him he knew that these men were prepared to kill him unless he put his signature to the Magna Carta. So he signed. When he returned to his palace he was in such a fit of rage that he threw himself on the floor, screaming and cursing. But the Magna Carta was signed, and the power of kings was no longer what it had been before. The king was no longer all-powerful and had to respect the rights of his people.

The most important rule of the Magna Carta was that no one could be put in prison or punished unless they had first been properly tried and found guilty by a court of law. We take it for granted, but it was not so before the Magna Carta. People could be jailed and executed on the whim of a king without any trial.

Another rule of the Magna Carta was that the king could not go to war with another country nor raise taxes without the agreement of the people.

Of course, it was not possible to go round and ask every person in the land whether they agreed, and so there was a Common Council as it was called, a group of people who could speak for the whole country and agree or disagree with the king. Without this Common Council the king could do nothing.

This Common Council was the beginning of Britain's Parliament. At first only noblemen and bishops were in this Common Council, but later the city merchants came and, in the end, people from all walks of life could be elected for it.

So the present form of government had its first beginnings with the Magna Carta signed by King John at Runnymede in 1215.

Of course, it took many centuries until Britain's form of government came about, and quite a number of kings tried to do away with the rules of the Magna Carta in the meantime, but they never succeeded. It remained the charter of freedom. For the first time since the Roman Republic people had a say in the ruling of their land.

7. Scotland and England

Freedom began in the cities where serfs and villagers could become free men. Then the king, the pinnacle of the feudal system, was forced to sign the Magna Carta, and so more freedom came to all people of England. But all this was only the first step on the path to freedom. We now come to whole nations fighting for their freedom against foreign invaders who oppressed them. And one of these nations was Scotland.

In Roman times, warlike tribes populated Scotland: dominated by the Picts and the Scots, who had come from Ireland. Christianity came to these fierce warriors of the north around AD 400, and the first to teach Christianity in this region was Ninian, who built a church and monastery in Galloway. But the greatest work in bringing the message of Christ to Scotland was done by Columba. From the monastery on the island of Iona, he and his helpers travelled from tribe to tribe and did not rest until all Picts and Scots had become Christians.

Later still the Picts and Scots became one nation, but they lost some of their land to the Vikings who came and settled on the northern and western isles around Scotland. In time, the descendants of the Vikings too became part of the Scots nation. The Gaelic-speaking Scots remained in the Highlands. But they were all now one kingdom.

The Kingdom of Scotland was on good terms with the Kingdom of England in the south. The king of the Scots, Malcolm Canmore, married an English princess, Margaret, who was an educated woman and had a considerable influence on ways of life in Scotland. More churches were built, merchants came who brought fine clothes the Scots had never seen before, and the queen set such an example of charity for the poor, and showed such gentleness and kindness that she was later called St Margaret of Scotland.

When the Normans came to England under William the Conqueror, the friendship between the north and south of Britain did not change. The kings of Scotland even invited Norman noblemen to Scotland and gave them land, so many of the later noblemen of Scotland were of Norman origin.

Scotland had become a prosperous country, at peace with its neighbour to the south, when a great misfortune happened. One dark night in 1286 the king who was then ruling Scotland, Alexander III, was thrown off his horse, fell down a cliff, and died. There was only a granddaughter to succeed him, and she was a little girl, Margaret (the Maid of Norway). Then she too died. Who was now to rule Scotland? The king who ruled England at this time was Edward I, the grandson of King John. Edward thought that he should become king of Scotland as well as of England for no better reason than that he was a distant relative of the little girl who had died.

A Scots nobleman called John Balliol, who had in the meantime been crowned as King as Scotland, gave up when the English armies invaded Scotland. The Scots suddenly saw their country overrun by the English, and in a few weeks Edward had Scotland at his mercy. He left English troops in different parts of Scotland to keep the people in order, and returned to England, well pleased with his easy success. But the Scots had not given up. A brave Scots knight, William Wallace, gathered men who were willing to fight for the freedom of Scotland, and they began to attack the castles and fortresses held by the English troops. Stronghold after stronghold was taken.

King Edward was not going to let the Scots shake off the English yoke so easily. He came with a great army from the south and took a terrible revenge, destroying villages and cities and leaving a trail of ruin and death.

Wallace had no army strong enough and he was defeated at the Battle of Falkirk in 1298. His men scattered and Wallace himself became a hunted man with no home but the wild hills. He found shelter among the Highland crofters, but he could stay nowhere for long. King Edward had promised a great reward for his capture and not only the English soldiers, but also some treacherous Scots were eager to gain the prize. In the end a Scotsman betrayed Wallace and he was taken by the English, brought to London and cruelly put to death.

But if King Edward thought this was the end of the Scots' fight for freedom, he was mistaken. A new leader rose among the Scots, a nobleman called Robert the Bruce. At first, only a few knights came to his side, but in 1306 they crowned Bruce king of Scotland on the ancient Stone of Destiny at Scone Palace.

Things went badly for the new king of Scotland. His army was defeated by the English and, like Wallace, Bruce and his few companions had to flee to the Highlands, where they were hunted from place to place with a price on their heads.

Many a time Bruce was so downhearted that he thought it would be better to surrender to the English. But some say that one day he saw a little spider trying to climb up one silken strand of its web – failing and trying, failing and trying – until, at last it succeeded. Seeing how the little spider had not given up, he decided he too would not give up and go on trying to fight the English.

As time went by, more and more Scotsmen, knights and common people came and joined Bruce. The time soon came when Bruce was no longer in hiding but led his Scots armies against the English. Eight years after the coronation of Robert the Bruce, the English were driven from Scotland.

King Edward had died, but his son, Edward II, gathered a tremendous army and marched to Scotland. There then followed one of the most famous battles in Scots history: the Battle of Bannockburn in 1314 at midsummer. The English were utterly defeated. They left thousands of dead and the survivors fled in terror. After this the English gave up the idea of conquering Scotland. The peace and friendship that once existed between the two kingdoms had gone.

In 1320, there was a great gathering of Scotsmen at Arbroath and on this occasion they sent a message to the Pope in which they said: 'We have not been fighting for glory or for riches, but for that freedom which to every good man is as dear as his life.' Freedom had come to mean to people as much as life.

William Wallace and Robert the Bruce (whose statues stand on either side of the entrance gate of Edinburgh Castle) are to be remembered not only as valiant Scots, but as fighters for freedom.

8. England and France, Joan of Arc

The story of William Wallace and Robert the Bruce shows how freedom came to mean more and more to people. But all this was still only the beginning. In those early days it was quite possible for people to demand freedom for themselves, but not to respect the freedom of others. The English had made King John sign the Magna Carta; they were not going to be oppressed and ill-treated by a king. But even though they had gained some freedom for themselves, they did not respect the freedom of other nations. They had oppressed the Scots, and only after years of war and the Battle of Bannockburn had they learnt that other nations too loved their freedom.

But even after Bannockburn, the English had not taken this lesson to heart. If England could not make conquests in the north, there was another possibility to the south, across the Channel, in France. The war between England and France lasted a hundred years, and so is called the Hundred Years' War.

In this Hundred Years' War the English had many advantages. Firstly, they were in England, in the land of the Magna Carta, where a great number of free men owned their own land. These free men, called yeomen, were just as keen to fight, to plunder and to gain riches through war as were the knights and noblemen. These yeomen brought with them a terrifying weapon: the longbow. The longbow was as tall as a man, and an arrow shot from this great bow had such force that it could pierce the strongest armour.

In France, it was different. There were no free peasants, there were still only villagers and serfs who had little or no training with any weapon and so, if their lords, the knights, used them as soldiers, they were not very effective.

Another thing in favour of the English was this: since the Magna Carta no English king could go to war without the agreement of the people. But the people of England were in favour of a war against France, for they hoped to gain riches and wealth through the conquest.

The people of France, however, had no say in these things. They fought because they were told to fight, and they had to fight for kings and noblemen who cared little for the common people. A French knight looked down on anybody who was not of noble birth. This again did not make good soldiers of the peasants.

Thirty years after the wars with Scotland had come to an end, the long war, the Hundred Years' War, between England and France started. It began – like the Scottish war – when the king of France died and left no heir. Again the king of England, then King Edward III, claimed that, by some distant relationship, he was the rightful successor.

But the French did not agree, and so war was declared. The English crossed the Channel in their ships, and already, in the first battle, the yeomen's arrows brought down so many French knights that the surviving French army fled. The English now went from town to town, burning and plundering. But France is a large country and new armies were sent to stop the English.

Then the fighting came to a stop. A new enemy had appeared that killed indiscriminately, Frenchmen and Englishmen, knights and peasants, men and women. It was an epidemic called the Black Death or Black Plague. It came from Asia, perhaps carried to Europe by sailors or pilgrims. But whatever brought the plague to Europe, it was a terrible disease. People struck by it died within two or three days with terrible black sores on their skins. In two years about half the population of Germany, Italy, France and Britain died. In some villages out of a hundred people only five or six survived.

When this terrible pestilence had gone Europe was in such a poor state that no one could think of waging war. But the war between England and France had not ended, it was only postponed. And forty years after the Black Death, England felt it was time to continue with the war.

Once again, the English began with a great victory at Agincourt, where English bowmen killed great numbers of French knights. By the year 1429 the whole north of France was in the hands of the English.

One of the most powerful noblemen of France, the duke of Burgundy, who commanded a large army, had gone over to the English and fought on their side.

The king of France, who was chosen by the noblemen, had died. His son, Charles, could not even become king because according to the laws of France, he could only become king by being crowned in the great cathedral of the city of Rheims, and this city was in the possession of the English.

Charles could therefore not call himself king, but only crown-prince, or as the French called it, dauphin.

This Dauphin Charles was neither very brave nor very clever. He was a weak youngster who planned to flee to Scotland, and let the English take France.

At this moment, when the French noblemen and the French dauphin had given up all hope, when nothing but a miracle could save France, a miracle did happen. It was not a valiant knight who saved France, not even a brave man, but a girl, a humble peasant girl: Joan of Arc.

Joan was a simple, good-natured girl who had no ambition to do great deeds. She loved her country and was sad to see it devastated by the English invaders, but it would not have occurred to her that she could do anything about it. It was not her own wish but a message from a higher world that made her do things that amazed everybody. She saw the Archangel Michael and he commanded her to go and help the dauphin, and to help France.

It was with the utmost difficulty that she reached the dauphin, and it was even harder to convince him and his knights that she, a peasant girl, was chosen to drive the English from France. She finally did convince them, and, dressed and armed like a knight, she led France into battle.

From the moment this uneducated, untrained girl took command, the English lost battle after battle. She took Rheims, and Charles was duly crowned king. She then continued the fight, but by now some French leaders were jealous of the success of this strange girl and they arranged for her to be taken prisoner by the duke of Burgundy, who promptly handed her over to his English allies.

The English could only believe that Joan had gained her victories by witchcraft and that she had been helped by the devil. As a witch she was condemned to be burnt at the stake. When the flames rose around her, Joan asked piteously for a cross to give her strength. A common English soldier had the kindness to pick up a stick, break it in two, bind the pieces together in a rough cross and hand it to Joan. As the flames hid her from sight, another English soldier said, 'We are lost – we have burned a saint.'

He was right. The English had lost. A new spirit had been born among the French and in the end the English were driven from France. Joan of Arc was later recognised as a true saint.

9. Printing and Gunpowder

A simple peasant girl, Joan of Arc, saved France from the English. Although she was burnt at the stake before the English were driven out, she had brought a new spirit to the French and, in the end, the English were expelled from France. Yet the English should really be grateful to Joan of Arc. If the English *had* conquered France, which was not only a bigger country but also richer, French influences would have become strong in England. And, as France was a rich country, there was no reason for the French to venture out to sea in search of wealth; the French had no need to become great sailors, or to seek their fortune overseas. If England and France had been *one* kingdom, the English might not have bothered much about setting out on great sea voyages either. The English might never have become a seafaring nation.

The spirit of freedom grew in Europe, passing from the cities to the men who wrote the Magna Carta, to William Wallace and King Robert the Bruce who fought for Scotland's freedom, and to Joan of Arc who fought for freedom against a foreign invader. But this spirit of freedom, this new spirit in Europe, not only showed itself in wars and battles, but also in the minds of people.

Before the Crusades, people in Europe would not have dreamed of trying something new. Everybody did what their fathers and grandfathers had done before them, and they thought like their forefathers had thought. A man was as much under the spell of his forefather's ideas as a serf was under the power of his lord. But all this changed now. New ideas and new inventions were eagerly taken up, and some of the inventions that came at that time changed life completely.

The Chinese had already invented printing. They used to

carve words of a page on a piece of wood (in mirror writing), ink it and press it on paper (which was also a Chinese invention). This kind of printing soon became known in Europe, but it was awkward to carve a whole book on blocks of wood, so no one in Europe used it for printing books. It was used for something else: printing the pictures on playing cards. Playing cards were printed from wooden blocks, but books were written by hand with quills. It took at least a year to copy a book like the Bible.

In Mainz, Germany, a man called Johann Gutenberg, who at the time was involved in making polished metal mirrors, began to think about printing books. It occurred to him that it would be simpler to make little blocks of wood, one block for one letter, and to put these blocks together into words until they filled the frame of a whole page, then you could print the page.

Then you took the letters apart and put them together again for the next page. There was no need to carve every page: once you had twenty to thirty carvings of each letter you need do no more carving, you just moved them round for the next page.

This was a brilliant idea. Later Johann Gutenberg had another bright idea. Instead of using wood, which soon wore out requiring a new carving to be made, a slow and difficult task, he would use metal. Lead melts easily, almost as easily as wax. Gutenberg made a copper mould for each letter and if he wanted a few more As or Bs, he poured molten lead into the mould, let it cool down, and there was his *type*, as it is called. If the lead type became worn out, it could be melted and recast.

The third bright idea he had was not to press the frame to the paper by hand, which always smudged the print. Instead he built something that evenly pressed the paper to the frame, which was called a 'press'.

Now he could print a hundred copies of the first page, re-arrange the letters in the frame for the next page, print a hundred copies of that page, and so on. He could print a hundred copies of one book in about three weeks or less. By hand a hundred writers would have worked a whole year to produce as many copies, or one writer a hundred years! Now one man could do it in a few weeks.

Johann Gutenberg had invented the printing press. He hoped to keep his invention a secret, so that only he himself could print books and get rich. But as he didn't have enough money to buy the paper, the print and the lead to start with, he had to find a rich partner who lent him the money. The partner had to know, of course, what the money was for, and as soon as Gutenberg had printed his first book, a beautiful Bible, the partner went and started to print himself. He employed men to help with the work who saw how easy it was, and soon people all over Europe printed books. Gutenberg died a poor man.

But his invention brought great change. Before the printing press, only a few people could afford to buy a few expensive handwritten books. Now there were cheap, printed books, and more and more people could afford to have and to read books. Knowledge became open to all who wanted it.

★★★

There was another invention that brought enormous changes, and we don't even really know who made this invention. The Chinese had already used a mixture of coal dust, sulphur (a yellow powder) and saltpetre (a white powder) to make fireworks. Perhaps the Arabs learned it from them, perhaps Europeans learned it from the Arabs. There is another story: an English monk called Roger Bacon had found, by his own experiment, that such a mixture, touched with a flame would explode with a bang. But he thought it was better that people should not know about such things, and wrote about it in his books in such a way that no one could understand it. Only much later, when people were already using this mixture, did they realise what he had discovered.

But there is still another story, although we don't know if it is true. There was a German Franciscan monk called Berthold Schwartz who liked to conduct experiments. He did not just experiment for fun; he was one of many men who were at that time trying to discover one of nature's secrets. How does nature make gold? But this Franciscan monk was experimenting with all kinds of things in the hope of discovering this secret. He had made a mixture of coal dust, sulphur and saltpetre. When he turned away to poke the fire in his stove, a spark of the fire fell on the mixture and it exploded with a great bang. Schwartz was badly shaken, but he talked about that terrible bang and how it had happened.

It was not long before soldiers realised how useful this mixture could be. They made large mortars (which were rather like long metal pots on wheels), filled them with gunpowder, put a huge stone on top, and touched it off with a flame. If the stone was thrown against the walls of a castle, it had such force that it shattered the wall.

These were the first cannons, and they brought about the end of walled castles as walls were no longer a protection. Soon people made thin tubes to shoot from, guns and rifles, and that caused the end of shields and helmets and armour, and when shields and armour went the knights went too. Once gunpowder came, the days of knights in armour were over.

In time, rifles, revolvers and machine guns appeared and made wars and battles more deadly than they had ever been before.

10. The Age of Discovery

A new spirit was abroad in Europe, a spirit of curiosity; there was an eagerness to find out things, to discover the unknown. The next great step in discovering the unknown was made in the Iberian Peninsula, the lands south of the Pyrenees, in Portugal and Spain. It happened while England and France were still locked in the Hundred Years' War.

Arabs had ruled large parts of Spain and Portugal for hundreds of years, since the early 700s. When Arab power was at its height, it was like a crescent moon stretching from the Pyrenees across North Africa to the Holy Land. But by the year 1400, the Arabs had lost much ground in the Iberian peninsula, only the south was still held by the Arabs, while in the north there was a Christian kingdom, the Kingdom of Spain. In the west there was another Christian kingdom, Portugal, and it was here that a period of history began which is often known in history books as the Age of Discovery.

It was one man who started the Age of Discovery. He was Prince Henry, the third son of the king of Portugal. His mother was an English princess, and perhaps he inherited his life-long love for the sea from her. Prince Henry was also a Knight Templar. The Knights Templar, who had been crusader knights, possessed great wealth, which they used to start new enterprises, for example mines for metal-ore. The greed of King Philip IV of France and of Pope Clement V destroyed the Knights Templar almost everywhere. However, in Portugal the Knights Templar survived and changed their name to the Order of Christ. Prince Henry was the Grand Master, the leader, of this Order of Christ, and as Grand Master he continued the task of the Knights Templar. This task was to strengthen Christianity, to weaken the power of the Arabs and the Ottoman Turks, and even more important, to open people's minds to the wisdom of the world.

Already as a young man, Prince Henry became famous for his part in a great land and sea battle in which the Portuguese took the port of Ceuta, opposite Gibraltar, from the Arabs.

But Prince Henry was not only a man of action, he was also a man of thought and of new ideas. The trade in spices had the merchants of Venice buying the spices from the Ottoman Turks. But the spices came from much further east, from islands in the Far East. The Turks brought the spices from India and became rich selling them to Venice. But if ships from Portugal could reach India, they could bypass the Turks and make Portugal rich.

But how could ships from Portugal get to faraway India? Today it is easy to say, 'Sail around Africa.' But at the time of Prince Henry nobody from Europe had ever sailed around Africa, no one even knew whether one *could* sail around it, no one knew how big or how small Africa was.* There was no knowledge, but there were strange tales.

If you look at the map you see a great bulge on the west coast of Africa. Such a bulge is called a cape. This cape was only known from hearsay, no European had seen it, but it was called Cape No because it was said that no one could sail beyond it. The sun, they said, is so hot there that all the water of the ocean boils away and ships get stuck in the salt. Even the bravest sailors were scared at the mere thought of sailing in this direction.

Prince Henry wanted the Portuguese ships to sail along the African coast and to find a way to India, but there was no map and nothing was known of the way. Even if one ship by sheer luck found a way, what use was that unless the captain of the ship could make a good, reliable map for others to follow.

So Prince Henry set up a school of navigation, the first of its kind in the world. In this school experienced captains from many nations, mapmakers, even Arab sailors and scientists, instructed the Portuguese seamen how to use the instruments

---

* In 1413 the Chinese had not only sailed around Africa, but probably also to North and South America, thus circumnavigating the world. When the voyages returned to China, a change of emperor brought isolation to China. It is probable that copies of some Chinese charts reached Portugal where they were closely guarded.

that show the latitude of a place, how to use a compass and how to observe the sun and stars with instruments, astrolabes, and how to make maps.

Only when they had learned all of this did the Portuguese ships set out. But they did not go straightaway around Africa. The first ships went only a short distance, then they came back and reported what they had seen. The next ships went a bit further and again came back with reports. And from these reports, maps were made to guide other ships.

Prince Henry received all these reports and saw to it that proper maps were made, but he stayed behind and supervised all this work. The Portuguese people laughed about him, calling him, 'Prince Henry, the Navigator who never goes to sea'. But later on they very respectfully called him only 'Prince Henry the Navigator'.

One of the earliest ships Prince Henry sent out ran into a storm and was blown westwards. They lost sight of all land and thought they would die of hunger and thirst, but then they saw an island, which they named Porto Santo. It was one of the islands now called the Canary Islands. There were no people on it, but the climate was very pleasant.

The ships came safely back to Portugal and Prince Henry sent Portuguese peasants to settle on these beautiful islands. They took seeds with them and soon their crop flourished. Unfortunately, the colonists also took rabbits with them. As there were no wild animals on the islands the rabbits multiplied and ate all the crops. The colonists had to leave. Soon another island further west was discovered, a large island that was called Madeira, which means 'wooded island'.

But these discoveries in the west were not Prince Henry's goal. He wanted to find a way south. His ships went further and further south, and from these longer and longer journeys along the coast of West Africa, they began to bring back things of wonder. They brought back ivory, which they had bought from the indigenous people for a few glass beads, and, even more exciting, was gold dust. Soon people not only in Portugal but all over Europe talked about strange faraway lands where the rivers ran with gold.

If it was not gold and not ivory, it was something else. The Portuguese sailors, seeing the African people, assumed that these black people were enemies of the Christian faith. They attacked peaceful tribes on the coast, took prisoners and brought them home to be used as slaves. So began one of the most shameful chapters in the history of white people: the African slave trade.

The ships went still further south, and some went up rivers into the interior of Africa. Every month brought new knowledge, new discoveries. But in 1460 Prince Henry suddenly fell ill and died; he did not live to see his dreams come true.

The enthusiasm, the spirit of discovery that he had roused in the Portuguese sailors lived on, however. They reached the southernmost tip of Africa, the Cape of Good Hope. They sailed around the Cape and, thirty-eight years after Prince Henry's death, the Portuguese captain Vasco da Gama reached India.

Within a few years the people of Europe began to buy their spices from Portugal, the Ottoman Turks lost their trade, and the power and wealth of Venice also declined.

But something much more important had happened. Prince Henry the Navigator had shown the world that ships could sail into unknown seas. He had turned people's minds to the High Seas and the unknown lands beyond. The Navigator who never went to sea had started the Age of Discovery.

11. Columbus

The news of the Portuguese discoveries, the news that ships had sailed to unknown shores, spread all over Europe. People's minds were stirred by these stories. In the old days people had some hazy idea that there was, far away, a place called Africa or a place called India, but no one had given much thought to what these faraway places looked like. Now it was different. Now there came tales of great riches, of gold, precious stones and ivory in these faraway lands, and everybody wanted to know more about these strange places.

Yet people still had very odd ideas about Africa and Asia. One can still see maps of that time that show Java inhabited by men and women with tails. Another map shows how cotton grows in India, depicting a tree that has little sheep hanging from the branches like fruit.

But these maps were very popular and people all over Europe wanted maps to see what the world was like. Map-making became a new profession. All this interest in faraway lands and in maps had been sparked by Prince Henry the Navigator and by the discoveries made by his ships.

Portugal's rivals, Venice and Genoa, were still engaged in the spice trade. Genoa also engaged in another profitable trade. There was very fine cloth made in Italy and the ships of Genoa carried this fine Italian cloth through the Strait of Gibraltar and then to England. The English paid good money for the cloth, and so Genoese ships frequently sailed through the Strait of Gibraltar and past the coast of Portugal on their way to England. It was not always a safe journey, because French ships made a habit of attacking the ships of Genoa and robbing them of their valuable cargo. There were regular sea-battles between French and Genoese ships.

In the year 1476, about fifty years after the death of Joan of Arc and sixteen years after the death of Prince Henry, there was one such battle between French and Genoese ships only a few miles from the coast of Portugal. The ships from Genoa were sunk and many of the sailors drowned. One young Genoese sailor, although badly wounded, caught hold of a wooden plank in the water and managed to stay afloat. For hours he drifted helplessly, but luck was with him and the waves flung him ashore on the coast of Portugal. The name of this young Genoese sailor was Christopher Columbus.

The Portuguese who found the shipwrecked sailor were kind and helpful. They looked after him and when Columbus had recovered he made his way to Lisbon, the capital of Portugal. Lisbon was very different from his home town of Genoa. Genoa's port was slowly dying, there was less and less trade every year, but Lisbon was a flourishing port teeming with vessels bringing spices from the East, gold dust, ivory and slaves from Africa. Sailors from many nations thronged in the streets. Columbus decided he would not go back to his own land, to Italy, he would stay in this prosperous, lively port of Lisbon. He was good at drawing maps, and so he settled down as a mapmaker. He did well in this trade and married a Portuguese girl, the daughter of one of the captains who had discovered Madeira for Prince Henry.

As a mapmaker, Columbus studied every map he could get hold of and one day he bought a map made by a fellow Italian, Paolo dal Pozzo Toscanelli. Now this Toscanelli had read the books of a famous Italian traveller, Marco Polo, who two hundred years earlier had travelled to Cathay – what the Europeans called northern China – visiting the lands of Kublai Khan. Marco Polo had travelled east to reach China and India. But this Italian mapmaker, Toscanelli, two hundred years later, had a new idea. If the earth was round, it should be possible to get to Asia, to China, to India by sailing *west:* if you went on and on west, you were bound to come to Asia in the end.

Now this is quite true. But this mapmaker, Toscanelli, made one great mistake. He had no idea of the real size of the earth, he imagined it to be much smaller than it really is. And so on his map the coast of China was only three thousand miles west of Portugal. The real distance is about ten thousand miles. But no one knew anything about the real distance at that time. When Columbus pored over that map of his fellow Italian mapmaker he had a great idea. The Portuguese ships were trying to sail eastwards round Africa to India for the spices. But this eastward journey was more than ten thousand miles long, as they had to sail all around Africa. But if the ships were to sail west across the Atlantic Ocean, it would be a journey of only three thousand miles – or so he thought. And he, Columbus, would be the first to open a new way to Cathay, a way that went west, across the Atlantic. Of course, Columbus himself was not rich enough to buy a ship, to pay sailors and to buy food for the journey. His dream could only come true if a king gave him ships and sailors to explore the great ocean west of Europe.

This ocean, which we now call the Atlantic, was in those days called the Sea of Darkness, for people believed that beyond the Canary Islands and Madeira, there was an endless dark fog in which no ship could find its way. When Columbus put his idea before the king of Portugal, he found that the days of the adventurous Prince Henry were over. The king had no wish to waste money or ships by sending them into the terrible Sea of Darkness.

At this time Columbus' Portuguese wife died. There was nothing to keep him in Portugal, and he decided to try his luck in the neighbouring country of Spain. So Columbus and his young son left Portugal for Spain. But Columbus' hopes that the Royal Court of Spain would be interested in his idea were dashed. He came at the worst possible time.

At the time Spain was ruled by King Ferdinand and Queen Isabella, and it was the Queen who made all the important decisions. Queen Isabella was the real ruler and she had set her heart on one great ambition. The southern half of Spain was still ruled by Muslim Arabs, and Queen Isabella, who was extremely religious, was determined to conquer the south of Spain and make it Christian. When Columbus came, this war against the Muslims was still going on. Queen Isabella told Columbus she would only consider his idea to sail westwards to Cathay when Granada, the last Muslim stronghold, had fallen.

So Columbus had to wait, and the waiting was not made easy for him. The Spanish noblemen of the Court despised him as a commoner, and the monks and priests who were the advisors of Queen Isabella were against his new-fangled ideas. They said to him, 'If you sail your ships around the edge of the world they will fall, you can never sail back again! You must be a fool even to think of it!' It was a very trying time for Columbus.

At long last Granada was taken by Queen Isabella's troops; the last Muslim stronghold in Europe had fallen and the whole of Spain was under Isabella's rule. But the war had cost a great deal of money and Isabella could not afford to spend money on a wild adventure. The ships sailing into the Sea of Darkness might never come back and the money would be wasted. Columbus was told to go and try his luck elsewhere.

Full of bitterness, Columbus decided to leave Spain and go to France or, perhaps, England. He had only gone a short distance when a horseman came galloping to call him back. A Spanish nobleman, Luis de Santángel, had offered to lend the money for the expedition. He hoped that Spain, like Portugal, would grow rich from the trade with spices, and that Columbus might find a shorter way to Cathay and India. It seemed to him worth taking a risk as Prince Henry had done.

It was this loan that made it possible a few months later for three ships to sail from Spain, perhaps the most famous three ships in the history of exploration. One ship, Columbus' flagship, in which he sailed, was called *Santa Maria*. Two smaller vessels, the *Pinta* and the *Niña*, accompanied the *Santa Maria*.

The day on which they sailed was Friday, August 3, 1492. It was a year that changed the history of the world.

12. The Year 1492

It was not only Toscanelli's map, showing the coast of Asia only three thousand miles west from Portugal (which is, of course, quite wrong) that made Columbus think of sailing out into the Sea of Darkness. There is a story that, as a young sailor, Columbus had once been to Iceland and heard tales of a land in the west that the Vikings had found and which they called Vinland. Columbus may have thought that Vinland was a part of Asia but, in any case, it was a story about a land not too far away beyond the Sea of Darkness.

Something else happened when he was still a mapmaker in Lisbon. One day a boat with two dead bodies was washed ashore on the coast of Portugal. These bodies were brown skinned. Columbus could only think that they were Indian people, which was a mistake, but he was quite right in thinking that this boat could not have drifted ten thousand miles, it would have sunk long before reaching land. It could only have come a much shorter distance.

So Columbus was right in one thing: there *was* a coast only a few thousand miles away across the Sea of Darkness. His mistake – and it was the mistake of Toscanelli, really – was to think that the coast beyond the ocean was Asia.

But even making this mistake, Columbus was still wiser than the 'learned' monks of Queen Isabella who said if he sailed 'down the globe' he could never sail 'up' it again. One day, Columbus got so impatient with their silly arguments that he said to them, 'You tell me my voyage is not possible. How do you know what is possible or not? Tell me, is it possible to make an egg stand on this table?'

'Of course not,' said the learned monks.

Then Columbus had an egg brought in and he set it so hard

on the table that the shell broke and was flattened and the egg stood.

'It *is* possible, and so is my voyage,' said Columbus.

In the end, his wish was fulfilled. He was given three ships to sail out into the Sea of Darkness to find China and India and to bring back gold and spices.

The *Santa Maria* and her companion vessels, the *Pinta* and the *Niña*, were the best ships of that time. These kind of ships were called caravels. They had three masts and three sets of sails (fore, main and mizzen) and could sail close to the wind. So to set sail against the wind they could tack, which means to go in a zig-zag course against the wind.

The caravels were a great improvement compared to earlier ships, such as Viking dragon-ships. But compared with modern ships they were very small. The *Santa Maria,* the largest, had room for only forty sailors, and the other two vessels carried only twenty-five men each.

They were also very uncomfortable boats. The bodies of the caravels were much rounder than modern ships and, being so small, they pitched and tossed like washtubs on the waves. None of these wooden ships was really watertight, and so the bottom was always filled with bilge-water, which had a terrible stench and was a breeding ground for cockroaches. Only the captain had a cabin and bunk (or bed) for himself; the crew had to lie down below deck in the stench and among rats and cockroaches. There was only one meal a day, consisting without change of tough, salted meat, dried peas and rock-hard ship's biscuits. Water was carried in wooden kegs and after a few days at sea had a brackish taste.

This was the kind of ship that set out on the most famous voyage in the history of the West in August 1492. They were not fast ships. It took them three weeks to reach the last known island in the Atlantic, Madeira, which had been discovered by Prince Henry's sailors. They only stayed a short while to take in fresh water, and then the real journey into the unknown began.

The first days were perfect. A gentle wind swelled the sails and Columbus kept a steady course due west. But after a week, by the middle of September, the ships encountered something that astonished and frightened the sailors. For miles and miles as far as the eye could see the water was covered with floating seaweed. The sailors, who had never seen such an endless area of seaweed, feared the ships would get stuck and would be unable to move backwards or forwards. They would remain there forever and die of hunger and thirst. The sailors fell to their knees and prayed to God, but their fears were unfounded. The ships sailed easily through the seaweed of the Sargasso Sea, as it is called.

After they had passed through the seaweed, there came other things to worry the sailors. A strong wind blew the ships with great speed westwards, and every mile further and further west they went, the further and further away they went from their homeland. Now the sailors feared they would be blown to the rim of the world. But Columbus quietened their fears and the sailors took new heart.

Three weeks passed. It was a whole month since they had last seen land. Never before had they been so far away from land. Columbus himself was now uncertain: according to his reckoning they should have reached Japan already, but on October 8 there was still no sight of land, only the endless ocean.

Columbus may have been uncertain, but his sailors were desperate. The captains of the *Pinta* and the *Niña* came on board the *Santa Maria* and demanded the ships turn back. There was no sense in sailing into the blue emptiness that stretched out before them on all sides. The sailors were wild with fear and excitement. They cursed Columbus, calling him a murderer who led them to their deaths. Columbus pleaded with the captains and with the crews. He asked them to sail westwards for another three days, and if they should still see no land then they would turn back and sail home to Spain. Grumbling and cursing the sailors agreed.

Now it seemed as if the winds wanted to help Columbus. A near gale-force wind rose and drove the ships with great speed westwards. Columbus hardly slept at all; day and night he stood on the deck waiting for a glimpse of land. The first and second of the three days he had agreed on passed. Then the third day came... and went. There was still no land. Then in the middle of the night, on October 11, Columbus saw the flicker of a flame far across the water and the news spread among the sailors. At 2 am the moon rose and a great cry went out: 'Land ahoy, land ahoy!'

In the light of the moon they saw a shimmering, white sand dune with hills rising behind it. The sailors cried and laughed and prayed and sang. No one slept that night.

When daylight came, the sailors saw a crowd of people gathering on the shore, shouting and talking excitedly among themselves.

Columbus was rowed ashore in a boat and his two captains followed him. He was dressed in dark velvet, with purple silk stockings, carrying in one hand a sword and in the other the royal banner of Spain. He was the first European to set foot on the new land. The crowd of people who had gathered stood and stared in wonder as these strange, white-skinned visitors knelt down and prayed. Then Columbus stood up and declared the new land to be the possession of their royal majesties, the king and queen of Spain.

The sailors cheered and then came and asked his forgiveness for their faint-heartedness three days earlier. Columbus thought they had reached India, but we know that on October 12, 1492, they had reached the continent of America.

13. America

The inhabitants of the island they had found were peaceful and gentle. It did not even occur to them to fight the newcomers – quite the contrary, they looked at them with awe and reverence. Having no clothes themselves, they touched the sailors' clothes again and again, wondering why these strangers wore extra skins over their own white skin. They brought fruit as gifts, and smiled happily if they were given some glass beads in return.

As Columbus and his sailors believed this island was off the coast of India, they called the inhabitants 'Indians'. The name was, of course, quite wrong as these people have nothing to do with the Indians of India. Today they are referred to as Indigenous Americans, meaning they are descended from the people who originally inhabited America before Europeans arrived.

But Columbus and his men were looking for spices, for precious stones or for gold. As there was nothing of any value on the first island, they soon left and discovered other islands not far away. They did find one island where the inhabitants brought them some gold-like pebbles, called 'nuggets'. The inhabitants showed them a river where such nuggets could be found amongst the pebbles. It was not much gold, but at least Columbus had something to prove that his voyage had been worthwhile.

He started on the return journey with the two smaller caravels; the *Santa Maria* had run aground on an island and was not fit for a long journey. In March 1493, seven months after they had set out, Columbus arrived back in Spain. The reception that the king and queen of Spain gave him was a triumph. Columbus walked at the front of a great procession, and behind him marched Indigenous Americans carrying gold ornaments and parrots. When Columbus knelt down to kiss the queen's hand he was invited to sit down beside her. He was appointed governor of the new lands and any others he might still discover.

Columbus soon sailed again, but this time with a large fleet of ships. Many Spaniards came with him, not as sailors but as passengers – they wanted to settle in the new lands as colonists.

Columbus put the colonists ashore on an island he had discovered on his first journey, the island of Haiti. Then he sailed on in search of further discoveries. He found a large island, Jamaica, and many smaller ones, but on none of them was what the Court of Spain wanted most of all: gold. When Columbus returned to Haiti, where the Spanish colonists had settled, he found the island had been plunged into bloodshed and fighting. The new colonists had no intention of working on the land or sifting the river-sand for gold. They had tried to force the indigenous population to work for them as slaves. They had beaten and ill-treated those who either would not work or did not work hard enough. Eventually the indigenous population revolted.

News of this uproar and bloodshed reached the Court of Spain. Queen Isabella was so upset that another Spaniard, a nobleman, was sent as governor instead of Columbus. The new governor asked the colonists if they had any complaints against Columbus, and when some men who had a grudge came forward and made accusations, the new governor put Columbus in chains and sent him back to Spain.

When the king and queen saw the great discoverer brought before them like a criminal in chains, they felt ashamed. Columbus was again put in command of ships and he sailed out to make new discoveries.

But from now on ill-luck followed him. The sailors and soldiers who came with him started fights with the inhabitants of wherever they landed. There was bloodshed on every island. Ill and exhausted, Columbus returned again to Spain only to find that Queen Isabella had died.

King Ferdinand had never cared for Columbus, and now that he no longer had any use for him, he refused to pay him for his services. Columbus, who was too ill to work and earn money, was not even allowed to see the king. He could only write letters begging the king for some money. In the end he was given a pittance, and Columbus died in miserable poverty. But within a few years his discoveries made Spain the richest country in the world.

When Columbus died he did not know that he had come across a new continent. But ten years after the death of Columbus, another Italian, Amerigo Vespucci, visited the new land and wrote a book about what he had seen. People were curious about faraway lands and the book was widely read. Amerigo Vespucci was the first one to say that this land was neither India nor China, it was a 'new world'. This new continent was named after him: America.

It is interesting how many Italians come into this story. Marco Polo told the world of Cathay; Toscanelli thought Cathay could be reached by sailing west instead of east; Columbus *did* sail across the Sea of Darkness and came upon a new continent, and Amerigo Vespucci recognised it *was* a new continent. They were all Italians.

However, it was not Italy but Spain that profited from discovering America. More and more Spaniards went across, driven by their desire for gold. Wherever they went they fought and enslaved the indigenous population, who were worked hard and given little food. They were beaten and whipped by cruel masters and they died in their thousands. A Spanish monk, Las Casas, was so upset by seeing them treated like this that he wanted to help them. He went to the king of Spain and suggested that Africans would be much stronger and work better.

And so the shameful trade in slaves, which had begun in the time of Prince Henry the Navigator, increased. Every year about a hundred thousand African people were captured on the west coast of Africa and shipped to America to be sold as slaves.

Las Casas, a monk, had helped the Indigenous Americans at the price of bringing untold suffering to millions of African slaves whose descendants, African-Americans, live in America today.

When Columbus set out proudly in the *Santa Maria* on that Friday in August 1492, he could not foresee what his voyage would bring to himself, to Spain, to Europe, to Africa and to the whole world.

14. Francisco Pizarro

Columbus travelled to America in 1492, which is not so very long ago in history. It was a time that already had many things in common with our time. The Vikings, who were the first Europeans to reach America (they called it Vinland), stopped going there when they found that it was already inhabited by people who resisted invasion.

At the time of Marco Polo, two hundred years earlier, only he and his family were keen to make long journeys into unknown regions. The Polos were an exception; other people of their time never went further than the Mediterranean Sea.

But at the time of Columbus people had changed. It was such a great change that from that time onwards life became quite different. Once it became known that Columbus had not landed in Asia but in a new continent, America, thousands and thousands of people were curious about this 'new world'. They were ready to set out and to try and seek their fortune in these distant lands.

How different from the people of Marco Polo's time, who had laughed about his stories but did not dream of travelling to Cathay themselves. After Columbus, people were ready to cross the sea and penetrate deeper into the new continent. There was something that made these adventurers very keen to explore the new continent. When the Spaniards landed on the east coast of America they found some peaceful tribes and some fearsome warriors, all of whom were hunters and nomads; they had no cities, no treasures. But from these people the Spaniards heard about great cities, far away in the west, where there were temples with walls lined with gold.

Men started to band together under a leader and journey through jungles, across mountains and rivers, enduring hunger and thirst, wild animals, indigenous tribes defending their territory from these new invaders, burning sun and mountain glaciers – all in the search for gold.

These men were called Conquistadors, which of course means conquerors. Hundreds of these Conquistadors perished on the way without ever seeing a glimmer of gold, hundreds came back, half-starved, in rags without having found anything. But some of them did succeed and found gold and treasures beyond their wildest dreams.

The most famous of these Conquistadors was a man called Francisco Pizarro. He had all the best and the worst qualities of the Conquistadors. He was courageous and utterly fearless, but he was also cruel and ruthless. Bloodshed meant nothing to him.

Pizarro began his career as a swineherd in Spain. There, on the dry, high plateau of Spain he looked after other peoples' herds of pigs. He never went to school, he never even learned to write his own name. But he was strong, and he thought he could do better for himself as a soldier in the Spanish army. So Pizarro became a soldier. After years of fighting in Europe he was sent to America and there he took part in expeditions against the indigenous tribes.

Being an uneducated man, Pizarro did not rise to a high rank in the army, he did not make a great fortune. But when he was fifty years old and had given up hope of further advancement and making a great fortune, he and his soldiers captured members of a local tribe who told Pizarro of a great kingdom in a land called Peru: the kingdom of the Incas. In this kingdom, so the tribesmen said, there were wonderful cities and gold was as plentiful there as leaves in the forest.

Other Spaniards had heard these stories before but were daunted by the hundreds of miles of dense, trackless jungle and the enormous, snow-covered mountain ranges that had to be crossed to get to Peru. But Pizarro was not daunted or deterred; he was fired with the idea of getting the gold of the Incas. He needed a band of men to come with him, but they needed equipment, horses, arms, and Pizarro had no money. So he persuaded another soldier, Almagro, who had money, to go into partnership with him. Moreover, Pizarro managed to obtain a promise from the king of Spain that he would become governor of any land he conquered.

And so, in the year 1529, 37 years after the discovery of America, Pizarro set out with 180 men. They had two small cannons and three of these men were armed with muskets, the first kind of rifle.

Between this tiny force and their goal, the Kingdom of the Incas, there stood the enormous mountain range of the Andes, with towering, icy peaks and yawning precipices. On many parts of this journey the Spaniards had to dismount and climb up the steep slopes leading their horses.

Had they been attacked during that part of their journey, they probably would have been wiped out in a few minutes, but they met no enemies. Finally, they reached the crest of the mountains and made a slow, dangerous descent. As they came down the slopes in the light of the setting sun, they saw below them the flourishing fields and gardens, the mighty palaces and glittering temple-towers of a great city. And, right in their path, outside the city they saw thousands and thousands of tents, the tents of a great army of thirty thousand Incas – nearly two hundred Incas to every Spaniard.

Yet this great army of Incas showed no hostile intent. When the Spaniards came riding down, their helmets glittering in the setting sun, their banners streaming in the wind, the Incas made no move. Instead, they looked at them with utter amazement. They had never seen white men before, or men clad in armour or mounted on monsters – for they had not seen horses either.

The vast army of the Incas watched with awe and wonder while Pizarro and his men found a little village outside the city that for some reason had been deserted. In that little village, the Conquistadors made their camp, and no one interfered.

The next morning Pizarro sent two officers with an interpreter to the king of the Incas in order to invite the king for a friendly visit. The two officers were just as astonished by what they saw in the great city as the Incas had been at the sight of the Spaniards. The Inca civilisation in Peru is something that amazes even today. They built towers and palaces from enormous blocks of stones, weighing sixteen to twenty tons, which had been brought over great distances, and which had been cut so accurately that when they were put together, they fitted so exactly that you could not push a piece of paper between them – no cement was needed.

Yet the Incas had neither rollers nor wheels for transport. They had not discovered the wheel, neither had they horses nor oxen. They had no iron to cut the stones either. The tools and weapons they had were made from obsidian, a glassy volcanic stone.

Their cities were bigger than any in Europe at that time. The wide, paved streets were so clean that the Spaniards' feet remained as clean as their hands. These cities had things no European city had at that time: pipes that brought fresh water from the mountains, underground sewers that took the dirt away. They had public hospitals and public baths with hot-water systems. And the people of the cities never locked their doors, for thieves or robbers did not exist among them.

All the land and all the food grown on the land belonged to the king, and the king's officers went around and distributed the food according to the needs of every family. There was no buying or selling and no one ever went hungry.

The king was regarded as a kind of god on earth – he was called the son of the sun-god. The sun was the highest god of the Incas, and the walls of the great temple of the sun were lined with gold an inch thick. The temple of the moon was lined with silver.

It was a high civilisation, but it also had its dark side. At great festivals the priests made human sacrifices – men and women were killed on the altars in honour of their gods. But the men and women chosen to be sacrificed never resisted: their life belonged to the king, the god on earth, and if his priests wanted that life they could take it.

And now this great and powerful king was invited by Francisco Pizarro, the former swineherd, for a friendly visit. This visit was to be the end of the mighty kingdom of the Incas.

15. The Fall of the Incas

Pizarro had less than two hundred men while the king of the Incas had an army of thirty thousand. Moreover, the king of the Incas had a personal bodyguard of two thousand. So it did not even occur to him that this handful of white men would dare do anything against him.

The name of the Inca king was Atahualpa. He was curious to meet these strange, white men with beards (the Incas did not grow beards) and who dressed in hard metal and rode on monstrous animals. He was curious and did not fear any harm from this little band. Atahualpa came the next day, carried in a litter by the highest noblemen, covered with plumes, golden ornaments and jewels. Behind the litter of the king came thousands of his warriors with their obsidian spears.

Pizarro sent an interpreter and a monk to meet King Atahualpa. The monk approached the king and made a long speech in which he explained the Christian religion, and he ended by telling the king he should become a Christian.

King Atahualpa listened politely, but he could not make head nor tail of what he heard about the Old Testament and the New Testament. He could not make out what this man wanted of him, and so he shook his head. This made the monk very angry. He held up a book, the Bible, and shouted, 'It's all written in this book!'

King Atahualpa had never before seen a book for the Incas had no writing. He took the book in his hand and looked at it.

'It tells you all,' yelled the monk.

Atahualpa put the book to his ear, then said: 'No, it does not tell me anything,' and he dropped it to the ground.

'Cursed heathen,' shouted the monk. 'Is that how you treat the holy word of God?'

At that moment Pizarro, who had remained in the background, gave a sign and with a crack of thunder his men fired their cannons into the mass of Inca warriors, killing hundreds of them. At the same time, the Conquistadors rode with their swords drawn into the Incas and cut them down.

The Incas were taken completely by surprise. King Atahualpa was torn from his litter and taken prisoner. In half an hour his noblemen and four thousand of his warriors were killed. Their obsidian weapons were useless against iron swords, and all the thousands of warriors were in such terror that they fled. They had seen thunder and lightning; they had seen their king, their god, roughly handled; it was like the end of the world for them.

King Atahualpa was in a daze. Who were these people who commanded thunder and lightning and who had put his whole army to flight? Now he feared for his life. He was willing to do anything the strangers wanted if they would only let him go.

To his surprise, he was told that what they wanted was gold. For the Incas, gold was not very valuable. They used it for decorating and ornaments; it was a beautiful metal, but not anything special. When Atahualpa saw the strangers were greedy for gold, he said to Pizarro, 'If you spare my life and set me free, I will fill this room where I am kept prisoner with gold as high as my arms reach.'

Pizarro could hardly believe his ears. He promised to let Atahualpa go as soon as the gold had been delivered. A messenger was sent to the Incas telling them what their king wanted, and for days they came laden with golden ornaments, cups, plates and statues, which they took off the temple walls and from their wives.

The Spaniards thought they were in a dream when they saw the room filling with the precious metal. As it would have been difficult to divide the thousands of different golden objects fairly between them, the Incas had to melt all the things down and mould them into gold bars of the same size. So many beautiful works of art were destroyed.

At long last the gold was all there, the room stacked to arms' height with gold bars. When it was done, Pizarro gave orders to kill Atahualpa. The king of the Incas was strangled in the marketplace before the eyes of his people.

The Incas without their king were like a beehive without a queen: they were completely lost and did not know what to do. The people who had killed their god-like king must themselves be gods. They looked at them with fear and awe and obeyed them blindly.

And so the former swineherd had become rich beyond his dreams. By treachery and surprise he had destroyed a great kingdom and become governor of the richest American colony, for that had been the promise of the king of Spain. But the time came when Pizarro had to pay for his deeds.

First there was trouble between Pizarro and his partner, Almagro. Almagro was not satisfied with his share of the plunder and some Conquistadors sided with him. It came to a terrible battle between the Spaniards, which Almagro lost. Pizarro, as governor, condemned him to death and Almagro was hanged.

But Almagro had a son, Diego, who escaped and was kept hidden from Pizarro's spies by some friends. Soon, more and more of the Spaniards came to Diego to plot against Governor Pizarro because he was as cruel to the Conquistadors who had fought for him as he was to the Incas.

One day, eighteen men, all sworn enemies of Pizarro, stormed into his house shouting, 'Death to the tyrant!'

Pizarro had some of his officers with him. They drew their swords and fought back, but one by one they fell. Pizarro held out longer than the others, but eventually, breathless and exhausted, he was killed when a sword pierced his chest.

Another Conquistador, Hernán Cortés, also with a handful of men, conquered the Kingdom of the Aztecs in Mexico. It, too, was a story of murder and treachery, and of a vast treasure of gold. The gold of the Conquistadors – of Pizarro, Cortés and others – went by the shipload to Spain and made Spain the richest nation in Europe.

Columbus had died in utter poverty, but his discovery made Spain richer and more powerful than any other country.

16. Magellan

The story of Conquistadors like Pizarro is certainly not one in which Europeans can take any pride. The Incas were in many ways more civilised than the Conquistadors, and all that the Spaniards did was to destroy this marvellous civilisation and turn the Incas into miserable and half-starved slaves. But how was it possible that such a great nation as the Incas, with an army of thirty thousand, could be shattered and enslaved by a mere handful of two hundred?

It was not the weapons that gave the Spaniards victory; the two clumsy cannons took hours to be loaded. It was not the swords, for one man with the best sword could not really win against hundreds of enemies even if they had no arms at all. Instead there were certain cultural differences that governed how the individuals of the two societies behaved.

The Incas lived in a highly regulated society where their leaders told them what to do and when to do it. The leaders distributed the food and all necessities of life for everyone, and all decisions were made for the people by a handful of priests and the king. Once the king was taken prisoner the Incas fell into disarray. The warriors would not fight without orders from the king, and once the king had been killed, there was in their mind nothing to fight for. They accepted the murderers of the king as their new masters.

The Spaniards were different. They were hard men, selfish, greedy, cruel, but every one of them was used to fending for himself, to fighting for himself and to making his own decisions. It was this which helped make two hundred adventurers masters of a kingdom of many millions of Incas.

Of course, this independence also has another side. It makes people selfish and quarrelsome, and it did not take long before the Spaniards fought each other. For us today the challenge is to learn to be self-reliant and independent, but use our independence *for* each other and not against each other.

Along with their plundered gold, the Spanish Conquistadors also brought back reports of what they had seen on their journeys. As a result, Europeans learned more and more about the continent that they had named America.

One band of Conquistadors, starting on the east coast of America, marched further and further west. After incredible hardships they came upon another ocean. They were the first Europeans to see the great ocean that lies on the other side of America, the Pacific Ocean. The leader of this band of Conquistadors, Balboa, had little reward for his discovery. On his return he quarrelled with a Spanish governor and was hanged for rebellion. But his discovery of a great ocean west of America inspired one of the greatest navigators and sailors in history.

This great sea captain, Ferdinand Magellan, was Portuguese, from the country of Prince Henry the Navigator. For many years Magellan had sailed on Portuguese ships around Africa to India for spices. The trade in spices was still very profitable for Portugal.

When Magellan heard that there was a great ocean west of America he thought, 'We Portuguese are still sailing east around Africa to get to India. But why should it not be possible to sail west, around America and over the newly discovered ocean, and so get to India that way?'

Columbus had thought he could reach India by sailing west, but he had come upon America. Magellan wanted to reach India by sailing west and going around America. The only difficulty was that so far no one knew where America ended, where there was a cape around which you could sail. But Magellan, who had sailed around the cape of Africa, thought that America must have a similar cape.

Magellan first went with his idea to the king of Portugal, but what had happened to Columbus also happened to him. His plans were met with a cold refusal. And so Magellan did what Columbus had done and left Portugal and offered his plans to the king of Spain.

The Spanish king, Charles V, was shown a globe of the world that Magellan had had made and then painted. He showed King Charles on the globe where, he thought, there was a cape in the south of America around which one could sail (of course he only assumed there was such a cape). Magellan explained to King Charles the advantage Spain would have, with not only the gold of America but the profitable spice trade with India as well.

In the end, the Spanish king agreed to give him ships for exploring a new sea route to India. But, as it turned out, they were not very good ships because the king had no wish to risk much money on such an uncertain venture. Magellan was given five ships, which were so old that another sea captain said, 'I would not dare to sail on them to the Canary Islands.' Yet it was these leaky tubs that made the first European voyage around the world.

Magellan set out on August 10, 1519, leaving behind a young wife and a baby son. The most precious possession he carried with him was his self-made globe. In the difficult days that lay ahead, Magellan would look at his globe and draw strength and courage from the sight.

The first part of the journey, the crossing of the Atlantic to America, was as bad as it could possibly be. The five caravels ran into heavy weather, there were thunderstorms and pouring rain, gale followed gale, and the ships were tossed about like nutshells. Something that nearly frightened the sailors out of their wits was that little flames of light appeared at night on the masts and ropes, running up and down and then disappearing. These lights, called St Elmo's Fire, are caused by electricity in the air and are harmless, but the sailors of those times were in great fear of them.

After two months of storm-tossed seas, the five caravels reached the coast of Brazil, where they had a short rest. Then they sailed further and further south, following the coast in search of a cape where they could turn west into the great ocean on the other side of America.

Only one ship had tried to sail south before, but when a few sailors had landed ashore to get fresh water, they had been captured by a warlike tribe who had killed them, roasted them and ate them. Terrified, the remaining sailors had turned round and sailed back.

Magellan and his caravels were now coming to a part of America, Patagonia, of which little was known except tales of horror. It was also drawing closer to winter in that part of the world and Magellan realised he could not sail on into snow-storms and howling winter gales. They would have to go ashore, spend the winter months on land and continue the voyage in spring.

17. Crossing the Pacific Ocean

The king of Spain had not been very generous with the ships he had given Magellan, and as the money he had given to Magellan to pay his sailors was also not very much, the crew Magellan found for his ships were unruly and unreliable. They were a mixture of Spanish, Portuguese, Italian and French sailors. There was even an Englishman.

When the winter storms came, Magellan found a safe harbour on the coast to anchor the ships. It was a bleak coast consisting of grey rocks with little patches of grass here and there, and nothing that could be used for food. Magellan knew they would have to stay in the harbour for four to five months and, as the only food was what they had on the ships, all men had to get by on short rations to make their store last.

But the sailors had no wish to spend months in this desolate spot with gnawing hunger. The captain and the crew of a Spanish ship mutinied, capturing another ship and breaking open the stores to feast on the ship's biscuits and wine.

Magellan sent messengers to the mutinous captain with the order to report to him. The messengers had swords hidden under their cloaks and when the captain refused, they drew their swords and killed him. After this the other mutineers surrendered. Magellan had shown that he was master of his fleet.

The crews had already been two months on this desolate shore where no sign of life could be seen, when someone appeared. In the accounts they gave when they returned, the sailors said that this man was so tall that even the tallest of the Europeans reached only to his waist. According to them, the giant was quite friendly, as were the other men of his tribe who soon joined him. The tall men showed by signs their great surprise that people as small as these sailors could build such big ships. The sailors, too, were surprised when they invited tall men to a meal. Each of the men ate a whole large basketful of ship's biscuits after which each drank a whole bucketful of water. Magellan gave one giant a little mirror as a present. He was so frightened at seeing his own face in the glass that he fell over backwards and knocked down four sailors who happened to be standing behind him.

Other European explorers who came after Magellan also reported encounters with very tall people, but it is thought that the original description of those Spanish sailors of giants twice the size of an average person was an exaggeration told for dramatic effect.

Unfortunately many of these indigenous people later died of diseases brought by the Europeans.

At last, after six months, the weather improved and Magellan's fleet went on its way further south. After a week's sailing they saw the coast broken by channels running westwards. Perhaps by sailing through these channels and picking their way between the rocks, they might come out on the other side of America.

Rain was pouring down, there was dense fog, and so Magellan sent one of his ships, with a Spanish captain, ahead of the others to see if there was a safe passage between the rocks and islands. But the treacherous captain used the dense fog to turn round and sail back to Spain. When the ship did not return Magellan thought it had run against a rock, and he spent days looking for survivors. He did not know that this ship had deserted him.

No trace was found and now the remaining ships wound their way cautiously between rocks and reefs and steep cliffs. Once they saw at night the flame of a campfire in the distance, so they called the land Tierra del Fuego, meaning Land of Fire, which is what it is still called today.

What made navigation between rocks and cliffs even more difficult were the storms that constantly buffeted the ships. But after five weeks they came out of the channels and onto a wide, calm, open sea. The sailors were overjoyed and they called this calm sea the Pacific Ocean, meaning the peaceful ocean. The strait through which they had come is called the Strait of Magellan after the navigator who was the first European to sail through it.

But Magellan was soon to find out that the calm waters of the Pacific would bring worse suffering than the stormy seas from which they had come. He set a course north-west, in the hope that they would soon reach an island where they could replenish their food, which was getting dangerously low. He could not guess how big the Pacific Ocean really is. After they had left the strait, the ships sailed for fourteen weeks without seeing any sign of land at all. The lack of food became desperate. What remained of the ship's biscuits was only dust mixed with worms, and the only water they had left was yellow and foul. Things became so bad that the sailors cut leather from the mast covering. The sun had dried it as hard as wood, so the sailors had to hang these strips of leather in the sea for five days before they became a little softer. Then they roasted and ate them. For a rat, men were willing to pay a gold coin, but there were not enough rats on the boats.

Diseases broke out and nineteen men died. Meanwhile, Magellan sat in his cabin and looked at his precious globe: it was the only thing that still gave him hope.

At last, after three and a half months, they came to an island. But there was an unpleasant surprise in store for them: a boatful of people appeared who climbed aboard the caravels and immediately began to steal everything they could lay their hands on. The sailors charged at them with their swords and drove them off. The people jumped overboard and swam ashore, leaving their boat behind. In the boat, Magellan's men found coconuts, fresh fruit, sugarcane and fresh water. This boat saved their lives.

But the hardest blow for the expedition came when they reached the next group of islands, which Magellan called the Philippines, in honour of the son of the king of Spain. The chief of one of these islands received Magellan very well. He made a trade agreement with him and even became a Christian. But this friendly chief was at war with the chief of another island, and Magellan offered to help his friend.

He went with a party of his sailors in three rowing boats to the enemy island. The sailors were armed with muskets and Magellan expected these weapons would drive their enemies to flight. They waded ashore, firing their guns, but the island's inhabitants were not afraid. They came in their hundreds and Magellan gave orders to retreat to the boats. Magellan was halfway to the boat when one of the warriors struck him with a spear. Magellan turned round and fought back, but a second man struck at Magellan's legs and wounded him. Magellan fell down into the shallow water where the warriors fell upon him and killed him. The great navigator died before he could complete the task he had set himself. It was now up to his captains to complete the voyage.

But their troubles were not over. The friendly king now came to the conclusion that the Christian god was not very powerful. He turned against the sailors who had thought he was their friend. In the end, one hundred sailors and two ships escaped from the Philippines.

One of the two ships was caught by the Portuguese, who did not like Spaniards interfering with their spice trade. The men were taken prisoner and languished for years in Portuguese prisons. Only four of them lived long enough to see freedom again.

Just one caravel, the *Victoria*, under Captain Del Cano, reached Spain, having completed the journey after three years. But of 265 men who had set out, only 18 returned. All the others had lost their lives on the long journey. The *Victoria* brought back a valuable cargo of spices, and her captain was richly rewarded by the king of Spain.

But there was no reward for Magellan. His baby son had died while he was away, and his wife died of a broken heart when she heard of her husband's death.

But Magellan's name will never be forgotten. His caravel *Victoria* proved something that before had only been a theory: that the earth is round. Magellan's little hand-painted globe was correct.

18. The Renaissance

The expeditions of the Conquistadors and Magellan's great voyage around the world were both signs that a new age was coming. But while the people of Europe began to explore the world to the west, the Ottoman Turks rose up in the east.

During the time of the Crusaders, the Turks had never invaded Europe. There was one thing that kept them out of Europe and that was Constantinople.

The city, named after the Roman Emperor Constantine the Great, was situated on the narrow strait between the Mediterranean and the Black Sea, and was like a strong gate stopping the Turks from advancing into Europe. Ever since the Crusades, they had tried repeatedly to take Constantinople, but had failed.

Although Constantinople was a Christian city, its people did not belong to the same church as those of Western Europe, who belonged to the Church of Rome with the Pope as the highest authority. The people of Constantinople did not recognise the Pope as an authority at all; the Emperor of Constantinople was at the same time head of the Eastern Church. Because of this there was no great friendship between Western Europe and Constantinople.

Around the time Columbus was born, about 1451, the Sultan of the Ottoman Empire, Mehmed II, swore that he would not rest until the crescent moon of Islam flew over Constantinople. He led a vast army of three hundred thousand Turks against the city and at the same time a Turkish fleet attacked from the sea. The emperor of Constantinople, who was called Constantine like the first emperor, had only fifty thousand men to defend the city.

In despair he asked for help from the Christians in Europe,

sending messengers to the Pope in Rome begging for help: perhaps a new crusade could save Constantinople. But the Pope was not interested in people who called themselves Christians without accepting him as head of their church. People who did not look up to the Pope were called 'heretics' and to be a heretic was considered worse than not being a Christian at all. So the Pope and the Christians of Europe simply ignored the desperate pleas for help that came from Constantinople.

When Constantine realised that he could not expect any help from the Pope, he called his people together and said: 'It is the duty of every man to give his life in the defence of his family, his country and his religion. You are now called upon to fight and give your life for all three.' Then he added: 'If I have ever hurt or offended any one of you, I am asking your forgiveness so that we shall fight and die as friends.'

Constantine could have saved his life and the life of his family, for the Ottoman Turks offered to let him and his family go if he surrendered the city without a fight. But he refused to save himself and leave his people, who he believed should at least have the chance to fight. And so for three weeks the Turks threw their whole might against Constantinople: their cannons smashed walls, houses and whole streets. But the people of Constantinople, the merchants, shopkeepers – men who had never carried arms – now fought with the courage of veteran soldiers. But they were too heavily outnumbered, and after three weeks the Turks broke through and poured into the city. They plundered and burnt houses, they killed Emperor Constantine and sold his family as slaves. The crescent moon of Islam rose over the churches of Constantinople and they were turned into mosques that remain to this day.

Now that the gate to Europe had been broken, the Turks crossed the strait and could reach the Balkan Peninsula. Soon Greece was conquered, and it became part of the Ottoman Empire for four hundred years. The Turkish armies swept onwards, through the Balkans and into Hungary.

Only when the Turks came to Vienna, the capital of Austria, were they stopped. Vienna held out against the Turkish advance and so saved the other countries of Europe from being invaded.

The danger of Ottoman invasion remained, however. As Europe had once been threatened by the Huns and later by the Mongols of Genghis Khan, so it was now under the threat of the Turks. Europe paid a terrible price for having left Constantinople to its fate. Yet some good came from the Ottoman invasion.

Before Constantinople was taken by the Turks, a great number of people fled westwards, mainly to Italy. These refugees from Constantinople spoke the Greek language and they brought with them books that contained the knowledge of ancient Greece and Rome, a knowledge that Western Europe had forgotten.

If this had happened three hundred years earlier, no one would have paid much attention to these Greeks from Constantinople and the knowledge they brought. But in this new age, when people's minds were eager and curious, the knowledge that came from Constantinople, the knowledge of ancient Greece, excited and stirred the Italians.

Everywhere in Italy there were still ruins from the time of ancient Rome: temples, statues and buildings. In earlier days no one had taken much notice of these ruins. If an Italian peasant unearthed a Roman statue with his plough, he broke it up and used the marble to fill a hole in a wall. But now all this changed. People realised that these things from the past were treasures. Bishops, princes and rich merchants began to collect anything that could still be found. An old manuscript from Greek or Roman times, or a statue (even if it had no head) became valuable and sought-after.

People also studied the Greek myths – the stories of Hercules, of the Trojan War, of Odysseus. They enjoyed and loved these stories so much that there were bishops who knew more about the Greek gods than about the Bible. And at the same time the Italian nation, from princes to peasants, became passionately interested in art, in painting, sculpture and architecture. In our time, thousands of people get excited about a pop singer or film star, but in Italy at that time the population of a city would come to look at an artist's new painting or statue.

This period when love for art and beauty was reborn, first in Italy and then spreading to all the countries of Europe, is called the Renaissance, which means rebirth. The Renaissance came at the same time as the great voyages of exploration, and it brought wonderful artists such as Leonardo da Vinci, Raphael and Michelangelo.

19. Leonardo: Childhood and Youth

The sixteenth century brought forth a blossoming of great genius. If a person had been born in 1500 and if they had lived to be a hundred, during their lifetime they could have met the astronomers Copernicus, Tycho de Brahe, Kepler and Galileo Galilei. The same person could have met Columbus, Magellan and the Conquistador Pizarro. They could even have met William Shakespeare and Queen Elizabeth I.

Of course this fortunate individual would have had to travel around a lot, and they would only have encountered some of these people when they were in their old age, while others would have been only in their youth. But such a person would have been able to meet people of genius, perhaps more than in any other century. And perhaps the greatest were the Italian artists of the Renaissance.

They were not just painters of pictures – they could do that superbly – but they also made marble and bronze statues, they were architects who could design churches and palaces, they could compose music and write poetry, and they had a thorough knowledge of geometry and mathematics. They even made new discoveries in art such as perspective.

In earlier times, the background behind the figures of a painting was very often gold. Before the Renaissance, a painting of Mary and the Jesus Child had no landscape or houses or anything in the background. These earlier painters used gold behind the figures to show that Mary and Jesus are holy, they belong to a higher world, the world of the spirit.

If any of these early painters did paint a house or a landscape it was without perspective. But the painters of the new age – the painters of the Renaissance – painted Mary and Jesus in the world we all see with our eyes, and in perspective. They discovered that, for our eyes, parallel lines come together in a vanishing point. The rules of perspective were only discovered about five hundred years ago by the great artists of the Renaissance.

It was a wonderful period in history, and one of the most incredible individuals was the artist Leonardo da Vinci. He was so called because he was born in the little village of Vinci, near the famous Italian city of Florence, and his name means Leonardo from Vinci. Leonardo's father, Piero da Vinci, was a rich lawyer and he wanted his son to also become a lawyer. But young Leonardo did not care to learn Latin, which was necessary for a lawyer. He preferred to spend his time in the hills around Vinci with a little book and a pencil, for he loved to make drawings of everything he saw: the waves and whirls of a brook, the fish darting in the water, the frogs in the reeds, a lizard sunning itself on a stone. All these he watched quietly for hours on end and made drawings of them in his book. It was in these early days when he was only thirteen or fourteen years old that Leonardo trained his eyes to observe accurately, and he trained his hand in the skill of drawing what he saw.

But his father was not very pleased with the boy who spent his time drawing pictures of frogs and lizards instead of learning Latin grammar.

Now one day a man from the village came to Leonardo's father and said: 'Look, Sir Piero, I have a nice round, flat and smooth piece of wood – a perfect circle – which would look well if I hung it up in front my house as a sort of shield with a nice picture on it. You, Sir Piero, often go to the city of Florence and know some good painters there. Would you be kind enough to take the piece of wood with you next time you go and ask one of the painters to paint a picture on it, something I shall really enjoy when I look at it. I don't mind if it costs a bit of money.'

Piero da Vinci was quite willing to oblige the man, and when he left, Leonardo's father put the round piece of wood in a corner to take with him the next time he went to Florence.

Well, young Leonardo with his sharp eyes soon discovered

this shield-like piece of wood with its smooth surface, and he thought: 'This is just made to paint on.'

He took the piece of wood up into his room and he spent a few hours making it even smoother until it became as smooth as glass. Now it was ready to paint on it. Now what should he paint? Leonardo took out his sketch book. There were drawings of fish and frogs and lizards and snakes. Which should it be? Then Leonardo had a bright idea: he was going to paint something that was a mixture of a frog, a lizard and a snake – he was going to paint a dragon!

Fired by this great idea, he set to work. For many hours he painted and painted. He copied the bulging eyes of the frog, the head of the lizard, the scales of the fish and the long curving and twisting body of a snake. When, at last, he put his brush down, a perfectly frightful monster glared at him from the shield.

Now this was going to be a surprise for his father. Leonardo drew the heavy curtains on the windows so that the room was in pitch-darkness. Only a slit between the curtains was left so that light fell on the painted monster; everything else was in darkness. When he had arranged everything to his satisfaction, he cried out with a piercing voice: 'Father, father, come up quickly!'

Piero da Vinci came rushing upstairs, wondering if his son had hurt himself. He burst into the room and had the shock of his life when he saw, in the gloom, a hideous dragon staring balefully at him.

For a moment he gasped, but then he heard his son chuckling in the dark room and realised what young Leonardo had been up to. He said: 'It will cost me money to pay the man for his wood that you have wasted. He isn't going to hang this in front of his house. But if you, my boy, can do this sort of thing, then you will probably make a better painter than a lawyer.'

The next day the father went to Florence and showed his son's picture to a famous painter called Verrocchio, who said immediately: 'If your boy could do such a painting, he is, indeed, a born painter and I shall be glad to have him as a pupil.'

And so Leonardo came to Florence as apprentice to this famous painter. But he did not start immediately with lessons in drawing or painting. Because you could not buy paint in those days, every painter had to make their own paint, and it was the job of their pupils to do this. The apprentices had to make charcoal that was needed for drawing outlines, they had to prepare the canvas for oil paintings. For two years Leonardo did only these jobs. Then he had to learn geometry and perspective, and when he had learned these things thoroughly he was still not allowed to do his own paintings. He was only allowed to paint a little part of one of his master's paintings – he might paint part of the blue sky in a picture, or a cloud, or the grass. It was a long period of study and learning for Leonardo.

20. Leonardo in Florence and Milan

It took years before Leonardo, as an apprentice painter, was allowed to paint a small, unimportant part of one of his master's paintings. But one day Verrocchio, the master, said: 'We shall now make a start with figure painting. I have finished this picture of saints and angels, except for one angel here, which you can paint, Leonardo.'

So, for several days, Leonardo worked on that one angel in the picture. When he had finished, Verrocchio looked at Leonardo's work for a long time. Then he turned to the young man and said: 'Your work is better than mine, Leonardo. There is nothing I can teach you any longer. You are a master.' And so Leonardo left Verrocchio and set up as a master painter on his own.

A painter could only make a living if people ordered a painting from them, if they gave them a commission. The people of Florence loved art, and a good painter could always be certain of getting commissions in Florence. Because Leonardo was a great painter, a number of people gave him commissions, but people soon stopped coming to him for pictures. Leonardo would start a picture, but then he would become interested in something else and would stop. As a result, the picture was never finished.

Don't think that the people of Florence did not like Leonardo, they loved him. Many people said that he was the most beautiful human being they had ever seen. He was excellent company, told amusing stories for hours on end, and on occasions entertained his friends with his great strength. He would take a horseshoe in his hands and bend it apart until it was a straight length of iron. Or he would tell his friends to drive a riderless horse through the street in full gallop, then he would step in the horse's path and stop it with one tug on the reins. He played a dozen musical instruments to perfection, and he invented some new instruments as well. One was a wooden box shaped like a horse's head with strings drawn across.

The people of Florence were proud to have such a gifted man in their city, but they did not give him any work because it was quite pointless – he never finished it.

Why was this? It was not because he was lazy – far from it. He could be seen working in his house deep into the night. He even invented a special light for himself to work at night, for there was as yet no electricity or gas. People had to work by the light of candles with flickering flames. To prevent the flickering, he put a candle in a glass cylinder and the glass cylinder in a bowl filled with water. The cylinder kept the flame steady and the water in the bowl magnified the flame and made the light brighter, as bright as dozens of candles. So Leonardo at times worked all night by the light of his invention.

Leonardo was so keen on inventing new things that, at times, he lost interest in painting. Although he could paint better than anybody else, he was, in his heart, a scientist and an inventor rather than a painter.

For example, when he had climbed the hills around Vinci as a young boy, he had noted seashells embedded in the rocks. Even as a boy he had wondered how seashells came to be in a place hundreds of miles from the sea. Now, as a man he thought of it again and he came to the conclusion that, once upon a time, the hills of Vinci must have been covered by the sea. At that time no one gave a thought to such questions. It took three hundred years until modern scientists came to the answer Leonardo had found for himself.

Leonardo also became very interested in human anatomy. He got hold of some corpses, which was not difficult in those days as criminals were often hanged. As there was no refrigeration the corpses must have smelt horribly, but Leonardo spent days studying these corpses, cutting them up and making drawings of the bones, muscles, hearts and blood vessels. His drawings are so exact and accurate they could still be used by a medical student today. Leonardo knew more about the human body than most doctors of his time. Another time he became interested in map-making and was, perhaps, the first person to make a contour map, which shows the height of the land. At other times, he would fill his notebooks with drawings of plants.

So Leonardo was very busy, working very hard. But with all these things to study and to draw he had no time to get on with the paintings he had promised to do, and that is why people in Florence no longer gave him commissions.

Eventually, Leonardo found himself without money and with debts; he owed people money and could not pay them back. Fortunately, Francesco Sforza, the ruler of Milan, engaged Leonardo not as a painter, but as a director of music and to make decorations for festivals and theatre performances. Leonardo did this work very well, inventing all kinds of complicated machinery so that actors seemed to fly over the stage.

Sforza was so pleased with Leonardo that he gave him a great and important task: to make an enormous bronze statue of a rider on a prancing horse, in honour of Sforza's father. (It was taken for granted that a painter was also a sculptor.)

Leonardo threw himself heart and soul into this work. It was to be the largest bronze statue in the world. He first made countless drawings of horses, then he made a little clay model of a horse and rider, and then he made a large clay model the size the statue should really be.

When that large clay model was finished, the prancing horse was twenty feet high, and the whole population of Milan came to admire it. To make the whole thing in bronze, Leonardo wanted seventy tons of bronze. That was a lot. Even the very wealthy ruler of Milan was shaken by the cost, but in the end he agreed, and the foundries began to make the bronze for Leonardo's enormous statue.

Just then the French invaded Italy and the bronze that had been intended for Leonardo's statue was used to make cannons instead. But worse was to happen. The French armies won and Sforza had to flee. When the French entered Milan and their bowmen saw the great clay model Leonardo had made, they used it for target practice. In a short time the clay crumbled and the whole thing became just a heap of dust.

So this was another great work of Leonardo's that was never finished.

21. The Last Supper

Some people are easily satisfied with their own work, they don't aim very high. They are quite happy if they can get away with poor work and little effort.

Leonardo looked upon such people with contempt; in all he did he set himself the highest standard. He would give endless time and unceasing effort to every task, whatever it was. But often people who did not have such high standards simply could not understand why Leonardo always took such an endlessly long time to finish his work. They could not understand that Leonardo was not easily satisfied and that only the very highest achievement was ever good enough for him, as can be seen from the story of the famous painting of the *Last Supper*.

When Leonardo was still working on that great clay model of rider and horse, the monks of a monastery in Milan came to him and asked him to paint a very special picture for them.

On a wall of their refectory (their communal dining room) the monks wanted a picture of the last meal Jesus had with his disciples, the last meal before he was betrayed and taken to be crucified. At this last supper with his disciples, Jesus said: 'One of you will betray me,' meaning Judas Iscariot, who was also present, although Jesus did not say who was to betray him.

This is the moment Leonardo painted. Jesus has just said these words and the disciples are shocked that one of them could betray their master. Every one of the disciples in the picture shows his horror or grief in a different way; only Judas sits grim and sullen and dark, knowing whom the Lord meant.

Even for a genius like Leonardo, painting this moment was an enormously difficult task. But he set about it with his usual thoroughness. First he wanted to find models for the faces of the disciples. For weeks and months he walked through the streets of Milan peering at people's faces. When, at long last, he saw a man whose face he thought could represent one of the disciples (although he is likely to have been Italian rather than Palestinian), Leonardo observed that man for hours until he could remember every feature of his face, then he rushed home to make a quick sketch of the face he had seen.

But sometimes months and months passed in which he could not see a face that was of any use to him.

The face of Christ was, of course, a very great difficulty. Where could he find a face to use as a model for Jesus? But, after many months, he saw a young nobleman whose face he thought had just the right balance between kindness and sorrow.

It was not only the finding of models for the faces that took such a long time. Sometimes Leonardo would arrive in the morning and stand before the unfinished picture in the monastery for the whole day, deep in thought. Then, at the end of the day, he would leave without having done a single brushstroke.

You can imagine that the abbot of this monastery became frantic with impatience about the slow progress of this picture. He pleaded with Leonardo to work faster and to finish it. He became cross with Leonardo, but it made no difference – the great painter took no notice of him.

At long last the picture was nearly finished; only one face was still missing: the face of Judas, the miserable traitor. Once more Leonardo roamed the streets of Milan searching for just the right face. He went to places where thieves and rogues came together, and filled his notebooks with sketches of their features. But none of them seemed just the right model for Judas.

By then the abbot of the monastery had lost patience. He screamed and shouted at Leonardo: 'I have put up with all this slow work as long as you had the excuse of taking great trouble over the faces of Jesus and the disciples, but I am not going to wait and wait for the face of that scoundrel Judas. Finish the picture immediately!'

'Well,' said Leonardo calmly, 'if you are really in such a hurry, I can finish the picture in a couple of hours. I shall simply use your face for Judas Iscariot.'

The answer shook the abbot. He was terrified at the idea that

his monks and the whole of Milan would see him painted as
Judas. And so he calmed down and let Leonardo finish the picture in his own time.

Leonardo's answer showed what he thought of people who
did not take great trouble over their own work and therefore
could not appreciate a person who did. They were no better
than Judas Iscariot, for every kind of careless work is really a
betrayal of the good work that is possible.

When, in the end, the picture was finished, people from all
over Italy and other countries came to Milan to see it. They
praised it as the most wonderful painting ever created. But here
again misfortune struck Leonardo, and it was his own fault
because he could not stop experimenting.

Unlike painting on canvas where one can use oil paints,
painters had always mixed their paint with milk when painting
on walls. Leonardo wanted to try something new on the wall of
this monastery. He used a special mixture of oil paint which did
not work out well at all. Only a couple of years later, damp
patches came out and spoiled the picture, then the brilliant
colours became dull, and in more and more places the paint
began to peel off. In the course of time the picture became only
a shadow of what it had been.

Later, other painters who were not as skilled as Leonardo
were called in to 'improve' the poor masterpiece, but they only
made things worse.

In the Second World War a strange thing happened. A bomb
fell near the monastery, and the whole building collapsed except
for the one wall bearing Leonardo's *Last Supper*. Recently,
modern methods have tried to wash away the overpainting of
the other painters and to restore Leonardo's work.

The *Last Supper* made Leonardo so famous that the city of
Florence called him back to paint a picture of a great battle on
the walls of the town hall. A battle scene with hundreds of men
and horses – that was a wonderful task for Leonardo! You can
imagine how he worked on every detail. This time he had
invented a quite special kind of paint: when you painted the
picture the colours looked quite dull, but when the colours
were heated they became wonderfully brilliant. Leonardo had

tried it out on cardboard and it had worked out very well. And so he painted this battle scene with tireless effort to show the Florentine people what he could do.

The galloping horses, the shining swords, the fighting men in this picture would be something that could never be surpassed. When the picture was finished the colours looked dull. Now charcoal-braziers were brought in and the glowing coals began to heat the painting. But a wall is not the same as cardboard, and as the heat rose the colours began to run down the picture; hastily the fire was extinguished, but it was too late. The whole painting was just a blur. Leonardo turned and left. Once again, his experiments had ruined work that had taken many, many months.

22. Inventions and the *Mona Lisa*

You may wonder how such a great man as Leonardo could ruin his first great paintings by experiments. But he was one of the few people in his time who realised that we can only learn from experiments. There was no one else who shared his love and interest for experimenting. There were no scientists who knew enough about chemistry or physics who could have given him good advice. He had to find out everything for himself, and he loved knowledge so much that he was willing to risk his wonderful paintings for the sake of an experiment.

Many people loved and admired Leonardo, yet he had no real friend, a friend with whom he could share his burning interest for knowledge. He was really a lonely man because he was so far ahead of his time.

When Milan was taken by the French and the great clay model of the rider and horse was destroyed, Leonardo first went to Venice. At that time Venice was at war with the Ottoman Turks. The Turks were storming into Europe after the fall of Constantinople and their ships attacked the Venetian ships in the Mediterranean, and so Leonardo turned his mind to inventing ways of defeating them.

In his notebooks (which still exist today) we find ideas that were only put into practice five hundred years later. He designed a one-man submarine to attack the Ottoman ships underwater, and a diving-suit with a glass-fronted helmet and air-filled bladders from which tubes led to the helmet so that the diver could breathe underwater. He thought of using gloves with webbed fingers for swimming underwater. These were used hundreds of years later by divers in the Second World War.

He had the idea that one could throw containers of arsenic sulphide at the enemy. Arsenic sulphide is a poisonous gas, and was used for the first time in the First World War. He also thought that one's own troops should be protected against the poisonous gas by a damp cloth bound over nose and mouth, which is the first idea of a kind of gas mask. He designed an armoured car driven by pedals (of course the petrol engine was unknown at that time).

But having thought out all these modern weapons of war, Leonardo wrote in his notebook: 'I will not make these things known for men are evil and might use them for killing.'

He did not tell the Venetians or anybody else of his ideas, but he kept them in his notebooks where he wrote everything in mirror-writing (so that it would be harder to read). Nobody bothered to look at these notebooks until the twentieth century when these kinds of weapons already existed.

Leonardo left Venice and returned to Florence to paint the battle scene that ended so sadly. But the battle scene did not matter so much to Leonardo for, at that time, a new idea had got hold of him: the idea of building a flying machine.

He bought birds in the market and set them free to watch how they took off. He measured their wingspan compared with their body and made drawings of birds in flight. Then he began to build all kinds of wings only to destroy them and start others.

He even thought of the possibility that the machine might fail in mid-air, and designed a parachute to save the pilot. His drawing clearly shows the same principle as a modern parachute. One of his drawings is of a machine that we now call a helicopter. The last of his drawings relating to flight is a glider similar to those used today.

It is fairly certain that Leonardo not only drew the glider but built it. He disappeared from Florence for a few weeks and when he returned he never mentioned to anybody what he had done, and his later notebooks never mentioned flying machines again. But in the countryside around Florence for centuries there was a legend that peasants had seen a strange enormous bird flying over the hills. So it seems Leonardo had tried out his glider. He was perhaps the first person to fly, but he kept the secret to himself.

We can see why Leonardo was a lonely man. There was so much he knew but could not and would not share with others. People had only begun to make machines like the printing press, they did not yet have reliable clocks or watches. Yet here was a man who thought of helicopters, gliders and submarines. People back then could not follow his ideas, he was just too far ahead of his time. They only appreciated Leonardo as a painter, but as a painter he upset and bewildered even his admirers.

Kings and princes begged Leonardo to paint their portraits, but he simply refused. Instead of painting these great and powerful people, he chose to paint the portrait of the wife of an Italian merchant. She was not a person of any great importance, but because Leonardo painted her, her name is known today all over the world, while the noble princes and great ladies of that time are forgotten. Mona Lisa was the name of this lady, and her portrait is perhaps the most famous portrait in the world.

This portrait is not large at all, but it took Leonardo six years to paint it. It became a portrait that shows not only the face of Mona Lisa but her soul.

By that time, the people of Florence had lost interest in Leonardo, who was about sixty years old. His battle picture had been a grandiose failure; if he painted a portrait it took him years and years, and he spent most of his time drawing machinery that no one understood. The Florentines turned their backs on him. Then Leonardo suffered another great misfortune. He had a stroke. His right arm was paralysed and he could no longer use it for painting or drawing. But this strange man had another rare gift: he was ambidextrous, meaning he could use his left hand just as well as his right, so from now on he worked with his left hand.

Florence was no longer interested in him, but the king of France was a great admirer of Leonardo, and invited Leonardo to spend the last eight years of his life in France in peace and without worries.

When people in these last years of his life praised Leonardo for all the work he had done, for the beauty he had created, he only shook his head and said: 'I have achieved nothing.' He died in 1519, the year in which Magellan set out on the first journey around the world.

Today we know that Leonardo da Vinci was one of the greatest people who ever lived: an artist, scientist, painter, sculptor, architect, engineer, and a seeker for knowledge and truth.

23. Raphael and Michelangelo

Leonardo had none of the cruelty and greed for gold of the Conquistadors, but he was driven by a thirst for a different treasure: wisdom and knowledge. A person who has one great aim in life, and pursues it regardless of anything else, is called single-minded. Just as the Conquistadors were single-minded about gold, so Leonardo was about wisdom.

The other great artists of the Renaissance were not so much concerned with experiments and inventions, they were not concerned with wisdom, but with beauty in art, in painting, in sculpture.

One of these great artists was Raphael. One thing that Raphael could do with ease that other artists, like Leonardo, could do only by great effort, was create the most beautiful paintings without making hundreds of sketches beforehand. Raphael made only a few sketches, but the loveliest paintings seemed simply to flow from his brush.

What he loved best was to paint pictures of Mary and the Jesus Child. He painted them again and again. Each picture was different from the others, and each picture was a masterpiece. One of them is called the *Sistine Madonna* (Sistine is the name of the chapel for which he painted the picture). This picture, showing Mary and her child in heaven above the clouds, and with the blue sky made up of countless blue angels, is perhaps the most famous picture in the world of Mary and the Jesus Child. Raphael was a painter who wanted to touch people's hearts, their feelings – not their minds.

Raphael, who could paint the most lovely pictures with ease, died young at the age of thirty-seven. But he left behind hundreds of paintings, far more than Leonardo who was thirty years older when he died.

Raphael was, perhaps, one of the most fortunate artists who ever lived. He was handsome, charming and everybody loved him. He was kind and gentle, and he made friends easily. The Pope, kings, princes and rich merchants gave him commissions. They gave him more work than he could ever cope with and paid him generously so that he never had the worries Leonardo had. His paintings gave pleasure to millions, but this happy life was also a short one. He died at an age when other painters are just beginning to become famous.

Quite different is the life of another great master, the painter and sculptor Michelangelo. He, too, loved beauty, but the beauty of strength. Most of the figures he painted are not sweet and gentle like Raphael's, but figures of might and power.

Raphael loved to paint Mary and the Jesus Child, but Michelangelo made statues of Mary holding the dead body of the adult Jesus in her lap. He depicted the sorrow, the tragedy of the mother who had to see her son crucified. Such pictures or statues of Mary and the body of Jesus are called Pietà.

Michelangelo painted enormous pictures of God creating the world and of God creating man. These pictures are painted on the ceiling of the Sistine Chapel in Rome. To paint these pictures on the ceiling, Michelangelo had to stand on scaffolding with his head turned upwards, and he had to do this for four years. He became so used to keeping his head this way that, when the work was finished, he still kept his head turned up, and had to read letters by holding them above his head. It took a year before he could hold his head normally again.

If you look at the works of Raphael it is like walking through a lovely garden. If you look at the works of Michelangelo it is like seeing mighty mountains reaching into the sky. In the work of Michelangelo everything is serious. But there was also little happiness in his own long life, even though he lived to well over eighty.

Michelangelo was not handsome like Leonardo and Raphael, nor was he gentle or charming. He did not make friends easily, he was ill-tempered and had fits of rage. He could work for months on a statue, and then, if it was not as good as he wanted it to be, he would take a hammer and break it to pieces.

We see how different three of the great artists of the
Renaissance were. Leonardo, the thinker and seeker after truth;
Raphael, gentle, sweet-tempered, whose paintings touch the
feelings; and the fiery, quick-tempered Michelangelo.

In Italy at the time of the Renaissance, there were not only
these three great masters, there were hundreds of artists,
painters, sculptors and architects who produced very beautiful
work. How was it possible that so many artists could flourish at
that time?

A few centuries earlier, in the time of the feudal system, the
noble knights could fight, but could not read or write and still
less did they care for art. The villagers and serfs were worked far
too hard and were too poor and ignorant to know anything about
art. Only the monks in the churches and monasteries had some
interest in art. The time of the feudal system did not give many
opportunities to artists. If Leonardo or Raphael had been born
three hundred years earlier, they could only have been monks
painting little pictures on hand-written parchment books.

But in the Renaissance in Italy there were hundreds of
thousands of people who loved art, who could afford to buy
paintings and could give work to all these artists of the
Renaissance. Who were these people who could employ so
many artists and who had the money and the time and the love
to enjoy art?

They were the 'citizens', the city-people: merchants, people
of business, bankers, lawyers, doctors. They were not knights,
they were not serfs – they were free citizens, and a love of art
was cultivated in the freedom of the cities that made all these
great masterpieces possible.

In the feudal age there had been only three classes of people:
the peasantry or unfree serfs, the nobility, which included
knights and priests, and the king. In the Renaissance there was a
new class of free citizens. They encouraged art and artists. The
great artists themselves – Leonardo, Raphael, Michelangelo –
came from this middle class. They were not noblemen or serfs
or priests, but free citizens.

In Italy, the feudal system had slowly withered away. In place
of the noblemen and lords the cities had grown rich and

powerful. But this freedom of cities also had its problems. Italy was not one country, but was split up into dominions of great cities. Each city had its own government and its own army or, like Venice, its own navy. And the cities were quite often at war with each other. When the French attacked Milan, neither Florence nor Venice took much notice. The city people were business people: they regarded another city as competitors. That is why there was so much trouble between them. But the free cities were the cradle of Renaissance art.

24. The Wars of the Roses

In the year 1453, Columbus was two years old, Leonardo was one, and in that year the Ottoman Turks stormed Constantinople and poured through the Balkan Peninsula in the east of Europe.

In the west of Europe, the terrible Hundred Years' War between England and France came to an end. Joan of Arc had been burnt at the stake twenty years earlier without seeing the end of this war, but it did come to an end. In 1453 England and France made peace.

In Italy at the time of the Renaissance each great city was a state, and the surrounding small towns and villages came under the rule of the big cities. The power of the big cities did away with the power of knights and lords; the feudal system withered away as the power of the cities grew.

In England things happened quite differently. England was very much a feudal state. It was the English knights and the English kings who had first tried to conquer Scotland and had been defeated by King Robert the Bruce. It was again the English knights and the English kings who had tried to conquer France and had been defeated by Joan of Arc. Both these wars could not have taken place without the consent of the knights, for the Magna Carta stated that the king of England could not go to war without the consent of his knights and noblemen.

In England, knights and noblemen were quite powerful; even the king had to ask their consent for taxes for going to war.

After a hundred years of war with France, which England lost, one might think that the people of England would settle down to a time of peace. The ordinary people, the peasants and merchants would certainly have wanted peace, but not the knights and the noble lords. But as they dare not attack either

Scotland or France again, they started a war among themselves, a terrible war with a beautiful name: the Wars of the Roses.

At that time when great artists in Italy created wonderful works of art, England was ravaged by battles between its own people, its own great lords and their knights.

How did this war come about? The middle part of England is divided by the Pennines, a north–south mountain range. West of the Pennines is Lancashire and east of them is Yorkshire. Now the most powerful noble families in the whole of England were the lords of Lancashire and the lords of Yorkshire. The shield of Lancaster showed a red rose and the shield of York a white rose.

The House of Lancaster had so much power that, during the Hundred Years' War, one of them, Henry IV, simply deposed the ruling king of England, Richard II, and made himself king. From then on, through several generations, the kings of England were of the House of Lancaster.

When the Hundred Years' War came to an end, it was another Henry, Henry VI of the House of Lancaster, who ruled. Henry VI, a king of the red rose of Lancaster, unfortunately suffered from what is thought to be a form of catatonic schizophrenia. For over a year, following the English defeat in the Hundred Years' War, he remained in a kind of stupor and was utterly unresponsive to what was going on around him, including the birth of his son. In those days, at his father's death, the eldest son of a king became king no matter how unfit he was to rule. And so somebody had to be chosen to rule England in the name of the unwell king. The man chosen was the duke of York – the House of the White Rose – the next powerful house in England. The duke of York was called 'Protector', but, practically, he *was* king and made all of the decisions. Of course, he gave all the high positions to his friends and to members of his own family.

Henry, although he was not very well, did not like it at all that the duke of York acted as if he were the real king. Henry's wife, Queen Margaret, hated the duke of York and did not want him to be in power. There were other lords and noblemen who were also jealous and did not want to be ruled by him.

In the end, all the enemies of the duke of York banded together under the sign of the red rose to depose him. All the lords and noblemen who supported the duke of York gathered to fight for him with the white rose on their shields and banners.

In 1455, two years after the end of the Hundred Years' War, the Wars of the Roses began, and they lasted for thirty years.

The duke of York was killed during this war, but his son, Edward, continued the struggle. Henry VI was taken prisoner and locked up in the Tower of London where he died. Queen Margaret asked Scotland and France, England's old enemies, to send armies to fight for the red rose of Lancaster.

Sometimes Lancaster was winning, during which time any noble who had fought for York and who was captured was executed. Sometimes York had the upper hand and executed the supporters of the red rose.

There was one lord, the Earl of Warwick, who first supported York, but when Edward of York had established himself as king, he turned against him and joined the Lancastrians. Warwick died in battle, but the war went on.

There was not only bloodshed in battle, but there was also foul murder and treachery. When Edward of York died, his son was murdered by an uncle who wanted the crown for himself. But the uncle did not enjoy the crown for long, he was defeated by Henry Tudor of Lancaster, a relative of Henry VI.

With Henry VII the red rose had won, and that was the end of the Wars of the Roses. To end the enmity between the two houses, Henry Tudor married a princess of the House of York.

During these thirty years of war, hundreds of knights and noblemen had died in battle or had been executed by one side or another. Their castles and the land they owned had been confiscated by either York kings or Lancastrian kings. When the war ended there were hardly any great and powerful lords left, and that was the end of the feudal system in England.

In Italy, the feudal system had disappeared because the city states had grown rich and powerful. In England, the feudal system was destroyed by the Wars of the Roses, although the king remained the strongest power in the country.

All over Europe, in one way or another, the feudal system, the power of lords, was breaking up. The end of the feudal system belongs also to this time, the age of discovery and the age of the Renaissance.

25. Borgia and Savonarola

At the beginning of this new age many new things came into the world: new inventions like the printing press, new exploration like Columbus' and Magellan's voyages, a new love for art was born, the Renaissance with Leonardo, Raphael, Michelangelo, and a new class of people became important, the merchant or middle class.

But as all these new ideas rose and spread, old customs and institutions were swept away. The feudal system with the power and the privileges of the noblemen and lords slowly withered.

For centuries the Church had enjoyed enormous powers and privileges. In the Early Middle Ages, when Germanic tribes destroyed Rome and its civilisation, only the monks could read and write and they made beautiful illuminated manuscripts. All these monks were sworn to obedience, they would obey the head of the Church, the Pope in Rome, in all things. If the Pope had decreed that the earth was flat, then it was the duty of every monk and priest to believe that the earth was flat, and not only the monks but every peasant, knight, merchant or king had to believe it. Anybody who dared to think differently and to say so was called a heretic, and a heretic was usually burnt at the stake. The astronomer Galileo only saved himself from the stake by pretending he believed the sun goes round the earth.

But long before Galileo, there had been all kinds of heretics, people who dared to have their own ideas about Christ or about how one should worship God. As these ideas were not what the Pope wanted, these heretics had suffered persecution and death. In the opinion of the Church, only the Pope could know what everybody should think, whether it had to do with religion or science. To disagree with the Pope was a deadly sin, a crime punishable by death.

But the Church not only had power over minds. Over the centuries, kings and lords and rich men had made great gifts of land, gold and treasure to the Church. They believed that if they gave gifts to the Church, they would be rewarded in heaven. As a result, the monasteries, the bishops and the Pope had become incredibly wealthy.

Some bishops had more land than the greatest lords, and the Pope had an immense wealth at his disposal. But all this wealth did not help to make good priests, and there were many who thought more about good food, drink and comforts than about serving God. That is why Francis of Assisi had founded a new order of monks, sworn to poverty and sworn to live without comfort. But after his death even his own monks went back to an easier, more comfortable life.

By the Renaissance, the Church as a whole had become as rotten as never before. The higher ranks, the bishops, the cardinals and the Pope, led lives that were a disgrace to the religion of Christ. At the time of Leonardo da Vinci, a man became Pope who can only be called a monster of evil. His name was Rodrigo de Borgia.

When he was still a bishop, Borgia was already known for wild drunken parties with his friends. Then the old pope died and the cardinals had to elect one of themselves as the new pope. Few of them would have considered voting for Borgia, but he bribed them with great sums of money and so he was elected as Pope Alexander VI.

But then he wanted to get all that money back again. This was not really difficult, for when a bishop died it was up to the Pope to choose the new bishop, and there were men who were quite willing to pay large sums to the Pope for the privilege of becoming bishops. Every time a bishop died, Alexander sold the vacancy to the highest bidder.

Unfortunately, the bishops did not die quickly enough for the needs of Pope Alexander, and so he found a way to speed up things. He used to invite a bishop to a banquet with excellent food, good wine and splendid entertainment. But the next day the guest did not feel very well, a few days later he was dead, and Alexander had another vacancy to sell. In the streets of Rome people whispered of a secret poison that was in the possession of the Holy Father. One had to speak of such things in whispers as it was not safe to speak openly. A young Roman nobleman, Orsini, spoke openly against the Pope. A short time later he was found stabbed to death in a dark street. Everybody in Rome knew that the Pope had a gang of paid murderers ready to do his bidding.

Money poured through Alexander's hands like water, and he always needed more. He thought of other ways of increasing his income. In those days people believed that the Pope could forgive sins on behalf of God. Someone who had committed a theft or even murder would fear that God would punish them for their crimes, but if the Pope gave them a pardon, then God would also forgive them.

Such a pardon by the Pope was called an 'indulgence'. It was a paper on which was written a pardon for a theft, or for a lie, or for murder. Alexander had the bright idea of selling these indulgences: people would pay so much for a lie, so much more for a theft and a still higher price for murder. Not only in Rome or in Italy, but all over Europe monks went about selling these indulgences, and people bought them. It was a great business that brought money flowing into the treasury of the Pope. But not all people agreed with this disgraceful business.

In the city of Florence, a monk called Savonarola preached against the luxury and wealth that had brought all this evil. He even went so far as to call Alexander Borgia a devil in human shape. Savonarola was a wonderful preacher. He had the power to move the hearts of those who listened to him, and soon the rich citizens of Florence felt ashamed of their own luxury. They made bonfires on which they burnt their fine clothes. They dressed in dark simple garments, they gave up their fine food and lived on bread and olives, and they turned against Pope Alexander VI.

At first, Alexander tried to silence Savonarola through bribery, offering to make him a bishop. Savonarola scornfully refused. The Pope found other ways to deal with the stubborn monk. There were many priests in Florence who were against Savonarola, and, at the Pope's command, they spread all kinds of lies about him, saying he was in league with evil powers. After a time, when the people of Florence began to miss their good food and their fine clothes, they were also willing to believe these lies. Once Savonarola no longer had the support of the people of Florence, he was doomed. He was taken prisoner by the Pope's men, condemned to death as a heretic and burnt at the stake.

But the justice of God that Alexander had mocked for so long finally caught up with him. He had planned another poisoning of an elderly bishop. There was the usual banquet, and a cup with poisoned wine was ready. But this time the cup-bearer who served the wine to the guests had been bribed by the bishop who knew what was in store for him. At the last moment the cup-bearer switched the cups, so Alexander drank his own poison and died a painful death.

When the people of Rome heard of his end they celebrated and danced and sang in the streets for five days. At his funeral they spat at the coffin and shouted curses.

26. Martin Luther

The story of Pope Alexander VI shows that this wonderful time of the Renaissance, the time when Leonardo painted the *Last Supper* and when Raphael painted his lovely Madonnas, was also the time when the highest ranks of the Church were filled with wicked men.

Yet the power and authority of the Pope was still so great that a sincere priest, like Savonarola, paid with his life for speaking the truth. There were hundreds of thousands of people across Europe who felt like Savonarola. They looked with horror and shame at the sorry state of the Christian Church, and felt powerless to change things. But then a man came who challenged and, in the end, defied the power of the Pope, cardinals and bishops. He was a German citizen by the name of Martin Luther.

Martin Luther was born in 1483, the same year as Raphael, and thirty years after Leonardo. He came from a poor family. His father was a miner who worked in a copper mine, but this poor miner wanted his son to have a good education. The parents made great sacrifices for their son and lived modestly to enable him to study.

Young Luther was a clever boy and became a university student. Even then life was not easy for him. To earn some money after his lessons, Martin Luther, like many others, went through the streets from house to house singing. Sometimes a door would open and a kind person would either give him a few coppers or a plate of food. Yet young Luther worked hard at his studies and at the age of twenty-one he received his university degree.

Then something happened that changed his whole life. He went for a long walk in the countryside with a friend. They started out in brilliant sunshine but later in the day clouds came up and the two friends were caught in a terrific thunderstorm. As they hurried to find a place of shelter there was a blinding flash of light, a loud booming sound, and Luther's friend fell lifeless to the ground. He had been killed by lightning.

From that day on a great change came over Luther. He asked himself again and again, 'Why was I spared? Why was my life not taken?' He became more and more convinced that God had spared his life for a purpose, and he decided to become a monk. In the monastery he would have liked to devote all his time to prayer and to the study of the Bible, but the abbot wanted him to preach sermons. Luther was afraid of giving a sermon, he was very modest and thought people would only laugh at him. But when he stood in the pulpit his fear of making a fool of himself disappeared. He spoke from his heart and all who heard him were deeply moved. In time, Luther even became famous as a preacher.

When the monastery had to send somebody to Rome, to the Pope, the monks thought they could not send a better man than Martin Luther.

When Luther came to Rome he was still a faithful son of the Church. For him, Rome was a holy city, and the Pope was the Holy Father. It was a great honour that he, a simple monk, the son of a miner, was going to meet this holy person, the Pope.

But Pope Leo X was not a very holy man. His main ambition was to become famous for building the largest and most beautiful church in the world, St Peter's in Rome (where both Raphael and Michelangelo painted for him). But all this cost money and Leo was as ruthless as his predecessor Alexander VI when it came to getting money.

In Rome, Luther saw priests, bishops and cardinals who used their position only to enrich themselves. He saw a pope who sold high positions in the Church to anyone who paid well enough, and all this was a bitter disappointment. But Luther was, after all, a monk. He had sworn an oath of obedience, and so it still did not occur to him to say anything against the Pope. He returned to his monastery in Germany and kept his sorrow and disappointment to himself.

The new pope needed vast sums of money to fulfil his ambition of building the most splendid church in the world. Alexander VI had found one excellent way of getting money by selling indulgences, selling people forgiveness for their sins. This shameful trade had stopped at his death, but now Pope Leo needed money to pay his architects and painters, and so he sent his 'travelling salesmen' into every country of Europe to sell indulgences. There were priests and monks selling forgiveness for any crime or sin.

The priest-salesman sent to Germany was called Tetzel. He was an excellent businessman. Tetzel usually set up a little stall in the market place of a town. He then made a speech and, as he spoke well, more and more people came to listen to him. Tetzel told them what a terrible thing it was to offend God by laziness, by telling lies, by using bad language, and what a terrible punishment God would inflict on all sinners. He had his listeners thoroughly frightened (after all, few people in the world can be certain they have never done anything wrong) and when they were well and truly scared, Tetzel said: 'But, my dear friends, you need not fear God's wrath and punishment. If you come and buy one of these papers here, each one is an indulgence by the Holy Father in Rome. Whatever you have done is forgiven by God as soon as you have paid me for the indulgence.' People queued up to pay.

On one occasion, this clever salesman Tetzel was caught in his own trap. A knight came to him and said he wanted to buy an indulgence for a robbery. That was quite an expensive sin, and Tetzel was pleased to get a lot of money from this knight. The next day Tetzel made still more money and when he left this particular town to start business somewhere else again, he carried with him a well-filled cash box. He was riding on a lonely road when, suddenly, armed men appeared, knocked him down and took his cash box.

'You sinners!' cried Tetzel. 'God will punish you for robbing a priest, the messenger of His Holiness, the Pope!'

'No, he won't,' said the leader of the gang, and he drew from his pocket the indulgence he had bought the day before from Tetzel.

Still this misfortune did not stop Tetzel and many other priests sent from Rome. They went from town to town, village to village, selling indulgences and earning money for the Pope and his ambitions.

Martin Luther had kept silent about his disappointment, about all the wickedness he had seen in Rome. But when these indulgences were sold like pills for headaches in every market square of Germany, he could not remain silent. He could not stand by and see people cheated in the name of God and the Christian Church.

He preached openly against this shameful trade. He wrote down ninety-five reasons why these indulgences were against anything in the Bible, and he nailed them to the door of his church in Wittenberg so that people could read them. People came and copied these reasons, and the copies soon spread all over Germany. Once people had read Luther's arguments against the indulgences the whole trade in these papers came to a stop.

The Pope was furious, and so the struggle between the Pope and Martin Luther began.

27. Luther and the Reformation

If it had not been for the stroke of lightning that killed his friend but left Luther unharmed, Luther might not have become a monk. He might perhaps have been a lawyer, and even as a lawyer he would have been against the shameful trade in indulgences, although people would hardly have paid much attention to his opinions. But Luther spoke against the indulgences as a priest, a famous preacher who had been to Rome and had seen the Pope. If such a man as Luther called the selling of indulgences a cheat and a swindle, then he must be right, and one could not simply 'buy' God's forgiveness by paying for a piece of paper. Luther's words had such a great effect *because* he was a priest. So the stroke of lightning that made Luther become a monk was of great importance. Without it, none of the things that now happened might have come to pass.

Copies of Luther's arguments against indulgences spread all over Germany. Because they were the words of a greatly respected priest, people in Germany simply stopped buying these bits of paper. As a result, Pope Leo X lost a large part of the money he had expected to receive.

The Pope was angry and he sent a letter to Martin Luther commanding him to come to Rome immediately. But Luther, remembering what had happened to Savonarola, was not going to Italy at all.

By now he was not just a lonely monk who stood against the Pope on his own. Thousands of people in Germany, who had been very unhappy about the greed and the wickedness of the popes, had been waiting for someone to take the lead. Luther was the right man and they all supported him. What all these people wanted was a complete change in the Church. The old form of the Church, with the Pope as head and highest authority, should be re-shaped, re-formed. As a little snowball rolling downhill becomes a great avalanche, so the argument between Luther and the Pope grew into a large movement of hearts and souls that was called the Reformation.

Having so many supporters, Luther not only refused to go to Rome, but he also wrote a short book in which he said that there was nothing in the Bible to show that anybody owed obedience to the Pope, and that the Pope was a servant of the devil not of God.

In response to Luther's book, the Pope sent a message to the town of Wittenberg where Luther lived. The message declared that Martin Luther was a heretic. He was no longer a priest nor was he even a Christian, and so he should not be allowed to enter a church or take part in any service. No good Christian should have anything to do with him.

In earlier times such a command by the Pope would have meant the end of Luther. But by now there was a different spirit. The whole town of Wittenberg sided with Luther.

Luther called the citizens of Wittenberg together and spoke to them with a power that moved them all deeply. He declared that he did not want to remain a priest in a Church ruled by such a wicked person as the Pope. From now on, he was the minister of a new Church, a Church that owed no obedience to the Pope and which had no master but God. The people cheered and made a big bonfire onto which they threw the Pope's letter and a good many other books that had been written against Martin Luther.

This bonfire in the German town of Wittenberg was an important event in history, for it was the beginning of the Reformation, the beginning of the great rebellion against the Pope from which came later all the other Churches and communities that do not recognise the Pope's authority. This bonfire was kindled in the year 1520, one year after Leonardo's death and less than thirty years after the discovery of America.

Pope Leo X had failed to crush Luther, but he was not going to let this dangerous rebel get away with it. The Pope now turned to the ruler of Germany, Charles V, and asked him to deal with Luther.

Charles V was a very remarkable person. He was the most powerful man of his time, and it was quite true what people said of him: that in his dominions the sun never set.

His father, Maximilian, had been emperor of Germany and Austria; Belgium and Holland were also part of his empire. Charles V's father was already very powerful, then Charles married the daughter of Ferdinand and Isabella of Spain who had no other children. Through this marriage, after Ferdinand's death, Charles V also became king of Spain. It was he, Charles V, who gave Magellan the ships to sail round the world. Apart from all the European countries that Charles ruled – Germany, Austria, Spain, Belgium, Holland – he was also the ruler of the rich Spanish colonies in America, as well as colonies in the East Indies.

So it is quite true that the sun never set on the empire of Charles V, for when the sun sets in Austria, it rises in Peru, and when setting in Peru it rises in the East Indies.

This mighty ruler, Emperor Charles V, was asked by Pope Leo to deal with that rebellious German monk, Martin Luther. The emperor was a fair-minded person, however. He did not want to do anything against Luther without giving him a chance to defend himself. There was also another reason to be careful. Charles V knew that a great many people in Germany – powerful lords, learned men, simple peasants, generals and common soldiers – were all in sympathy with Luther. Charles V was too clever a man to stir up trouble if he could help it. Luther should have a fair chance to speak for himself.

Charles V called a meeting of princes and noblemen, of cardinals and bishops, all the great and powerful men of Germany. Luther was also summoned to appear before this gathering and to defend himself. He was promised 'safe conduct', which means that whatever was decided at this meeting, Luther would be allowed to return to his loyal town of Wittenberg.

So this monk, the son of a miner, was to come before the most powerful people of his time, including the mighty emperor, Charles V.

28. The Diet of Worms

Emperor Charles V's assembly of lords and noblemen was called a 'diet', and the city where this diet was to meet was a German city called Worms. So this important assembly is called the Diet of Worms, which sounds funny, but it was not funny for Martin Luther.

There are many kinds of courage: the courage of a soldier going into battle or courage to own up if one has done something wrong. It needed a special kind of courage to walk alone, like Luther, into a great assembly and to defend himself before the high and mighty lords of Germany and the emperor himself.

When Luther approached the doors of the assembly hall, one of the soldiers on guard patted him on the shoulder and said: 'I've gone into many a battle without fear, but I would not like to be in your shoes, little monk.' Then the doors opened and Luther entered the great hall. At the back of the hall on a high throne sat the emperor, Charles V. To one side of the throne stood a Roman cardinal in his crimson robe, the Pope's envoy. Five thousand people thronged the hall: lords and knights in their colourful clothes, lawyers and learned men dressed in black, bishops, priests and monks. When Luther walked in, this great crowd fell silent and all eyes turned to this monk in his dark-brown habit.

Luther walked through the crowd until he faced the Roman cardinal. And now, while all these thousands listened, the questioning began.

The Roman cardinal, the Pope's ambassador, fired questions at Luther, questions that were meant to trip him up or to show his ignorance. These questions went on and on. Except for short breaks at mealtimes, the questioning lasted all day and went on into the next. The purpose of this long argument was to make Luther admit that he was wrong and the Pope right.

But at the end of it all, when the cardinal had no more questions, Luther said words that have become famous in history: 'I will not take back anything I have said for this would be against my conscience. Here I stand; I can do no other. God help me, amen.'

Emperor Charles V had promised Luther safe conduct, and so, when Luther had said these words with a ringing voice, he was allowed to leave the assembly and set out on his journey home to Wittenberg. Luther was still on his way when Charles V made it known that, after having listened to that long discussion, he had come to a decision. The decision was that Luther was in the wrong, that Luther was a heretic and that he was an outlaw. If a man was declared an outlaw, it meant that he was no longer protected by any law, and that he could be killed by anyone without fear of punishment.

Now that Luther was an outlaw his life was no longer safe. But he had friends in Germany, people who were on his side, and they helped him to go into hiding. Luther found shelter in a castle called the Wartburg where he was safe from his enemies.

While Luther was in hiding in this castle, he began a great task: the translation of the Bible into German. Up to that time, the Bible was only for educated people who knew Latin – the Church did not want everyone to be able to read the Bible. There was no Bible in German or English or French, there were only some stories from the Bible that people could hear from priests. Some men who had tried to translate the Bible into their own language had risked their life doing so.

But Luther, as a German, wanted all his people, not only those who knew Latin, to be able to read the Bible. So he used the time he was hiding in the Wartburg to make a translation. This was not an easy task. Even now, learned people disagree on how many parts of the Bible should be translated. There is a strange story about what happened to Luther when he was translating the Bible at the Wartburg.

He was always a hard worker, poring over his translation deep into the night. Perhaps he fell asleep over his work and only dreamed what he saw, but one night it seemed to him that the light of his candle grew very dim. A strange cold wind came from nowhere and made him shudder, and at the same time an unpleasant stench assailed his nose. Luther, who had not lifted his head from his writing, now looked up and saw before him a dark shape, like a shadow, but a shadow with bat's wings and horns. This black shape placed a dark, claw-like hand over Luther's writing, as if it wanted to stop him from going on with it. But Luther, as you have seen on other occasions, was not easily frightened. He was only angry that there was something that interfered with his work. He took the inkpot from his desk and threw it at the dark shape. As the glass shattered on the wall, the dark shape, the stench and the cold air disappeared in an instant. All that remained was a big splash of ink on the wall.

The Wartburg castle where Luther translated the Bible into German still stands, and visitors who go there can still see the ink blot on the wall made by Luther when he threw the inkpot at the devil.

After a year, Luther was able to leave the Wartburg, for the emperor was fighting a war against France and had no time to bother about a troublesome monk.

Luther returned to Wittenberg where his friends received him with joy. He could now work for the new kind of Church he had in mind: a free Church, independent of the Pope, independent of Rome. The new kind of Church was called Protestant, for the people who joined it protested against the shameful practices of Rome.

Luther took one more step away from the customs of the Roman Catholic Church. There was nothing in the Bible that said priests should not marry. It was a rule that had been made by Pope Gregory the Great. As the rules of popes did not count any longer for Luther, he put away his monk's habit and married.

All his life Luther hoped that the great movement that had begun would not lead to bloodshed. He died at the age of sixty-three and so did not see the massacres and wars that the Reformation brought about.

29. Calvin and Knox

Luther was not alone in challenging the authority of the Pope. Many thousands of people took his side who felt that the Church of Rome was no longer a true Church of Christ. These people supported Luther. But there were others who did not agree with Luther. They knew, just as Luther did, that there were evil popes. They knew that the selling of indulgences was a shame and a disgrace for the Church. Yet these educated people were more worried about Luther than about the evil popes. They said: 'Yes, there is much that needs changing in the Church, much that is wrong that must be put right. But this change should be made by good men who work within the Church, good men who are bishops and cardinals, and who might one day become popes. If rebels like Martin Luther break away from the Church and start a Church of their own, there will be no end of it. There will be all kinds of troublemakers, each one starting their own Church. They will argue among themselves and it will only bring trouble and suffering. It would be far better if we all remained faithful sons and daughters of one Church, but make it a better Church than it is now.'

That is why these people did not support Luther, for they did not want this breaking up of one Church into many. They foresaw that great suffering would follow from it. But they had no power and neither side was ready to listen to them. As a result, the terrible events that they had foreseen came to pass.

Once Luther had shown that it was possible to defy the Pope and the Reformation had started, there came other 'reformers' who were not only against the Pope but against Luther and against each other. Before the Reformation there had, at least, been only one man who claimed to know the will of God; now there were many. Each of these reformers had supporters and followers who formed a Church of their own, and all these different 'reformed' Churches were at loggerheads with the Church of Rome and with each other.

One of these reformers was a Frenchman, John Calvin. Like Luther he was first a priest of the Roman Catholic Church, and like Luther he was upset by the evil ways of the popes. When Calvin heard of the great changes in Germany, when he heard how Luther had succeeded against Rome, Calvin also left the Church of Rome and preached against it. But his own country, France, was ruled by King Francis who had no patience with heretics, and Calvin had to flee for his life. He went to Switzerland where he found a city that welcomed him: the city of Geneva.

After a short time, the citizens of Geneva made Calvin a kind of ruler whose word was law. What he wished and what he said was law in Geneva, and life in Geneva was not easy under Calvin.

Like Savonarola, he thought that luxury, vanity and comfort made people evil, and so the people of Geneva had to do without anything that was not absolutely necessary for life. The colourful clothes people used to have in those days were forbidden, only plain black was allowed. Dancing, drinking wine and playing cards were also banned. Not only that, but art was also seen as a kind of luxury, so the churches had to be quite plain without pictures, statues or stained-glass windows. Any amusement or entertainment was an unnecessary luxury and so was outlawed. If the people of Geneva broke these rules a number of times they were executed. John Calvin's Church was a very stern one.

In Scotland, too, the time was ripe for change. The bishops owned more than half of the country's wealth and the monks were so corrupt that you could hear anywhere in Scotland songs that mocked the sinful lives of the priests. Yet who would dare speak against the Pope? Scotland was not Germany, and the king of Scotland, James V, would not allow any heretics. If you had been in the town of St Andrews in 1528, you would have seen a bonfire that was quite different from the bonfire in Wittenberg. In this bonfire in St Andrews a young Scotsman, Patrick Hamilton, was burned.

Patrick Hamilton had been to Germany and he had heard of

Luther and the new Church that Luther had founded, a Church free of Rome. Patrick Hamilton thought this was wonderful and he came back to Scotland and began to preach – but not for long. He paid for his preaching at the stake in St Andrews.

But Patrick Hamilton's death did not stop the new ideas that were sweeping over Europe. The number of Protestants in Scotland grew, in spite of persecutions and burnings. They even began to fight back. One day a group of Protestants stormed St Andrew's castle and took Cardinal Beaton, who had been their worst oppressor, and hanged him from the window of the castle.

Both sides, the Roman Catholics and the Protestants, fought and killed each other in the name of religion, and forgot that Christ had said: 'Love your enemy.'

The Scots had always been good friends with the French, and so James V called for French ships to help him against the rebellious Protestants of St Andrews. The rebellion was suppressed and there was harsh punishment for the Protestants. One of them was taken to France and condemned to be a galley-slave chained to an oar under the heavy whip of the overseer, rowing with other poor wretches on a French ship. The name of this Protestant sufferer was John Knox. After eighteen months of this terrible life as a galley-slave, he escaped and made his way to Switzerland, to Geneva.

That is how John Knox met John Calvin, the stern ruler of Geneva. John Knox agreed with Calvin and thought that Scotland should have the same kind of Church and life as Calvin had established in Geneva. He was so enthusiastic about this idea that he returned to Scotland despite the persecutions of Protestants.

By now, not only common people, but even noblemen and lords took the sides of the Protestants. They made a 'covenant', a pledge to help each other and do all they could for the new faith. So many people joined the covenant that the king could no longer suppress it. John Knox, who was also a great preacher, brought more and more people to his side. He became the leader of the Covenanters, and in the year 1560 he had the great satisfaction that the kind of Church he wanted, a Church as severe as Calvin's, was declared the Church of Scotland. After much bloodshed, burning and suffering, Scotland had broken away from Rome and had its own Church.

Under the influence of John Knox, pictures, statues and stained-glass windows in Scottish churches were destroyed, and entertainments were abolished. But Knox did not execute people for disobeying his rules as Calvin had done. He also had education very much at heart. Due to John Knox, Scotland became the only country at that time where even the children of the poor could go to school and have an education.

As it was with many reformers, there are things one can like in John Knox but also things that one can dislike.

30. Henry VIII

The Reformation was, first of all, another expression of the change in the human mind that we have already seen in the various inventions and voyages of discovery, in Copernicus with his new idea about the sun and the earth, and in the Renaissance painters and the use of perspective in painting.

The Reformation came about because people no longer tolerated the old ways and the authority of the Pope. There had been some quite wicked popes a few hundred years earlier. There was even a time when there were two popes who stood against each other, one in Rome and one in Avignon, in France. Yet in those times, even when there were two popes, people still looked up to one or other of them, but they never questioned whether or not there should be a pope. Now people no longer felt that they needed or wanted the authority of the Pope.

There were also other people who did not want change. For these people, even a wicked pope was better than having no pope at all.

In the south of Europe, in Spain, Portugal and Italy, people remained faithful to the Church of Rome and the authority of the Pope. In these sunny, warm lands of Europe, the new spirit did not touch religion; instead people became explorers like Columbus or Magellan, or artists like Leonardo and Raphael. They used the new spirit for discoveries or in art. But in the colder countries of the north there was as yet little in the way of exploring, and art changed only slowly. North of the Alps the spirit of new things turned to religion and so brought the Reformation.

It was not the case in these countries that all people wanted a new Church, or that all people wanted to break away from Rome, and so there was a lot of suffering and bloodshed.

In Scotland the Protestants grew so strong that in the end the king, who was a Roman Catholic and who did not want the Reformation, had to give in. John Knox's ideas led to the Church of Scotland.

In England it was just the opposite. There the Reformation came by the will of the king. That is one difference between Scotland and England: in Scotland the Reformation came through the people, in England it came through the king.

These two men, John Knox and King Henry VIII of England, were also as persons the very opposite of each other. John Knox was of small stature and thin. He ate and drank very little, just as much as was necessary. Henry VIII was tall and overweight, and whenever he ate a meal he gorged himself. John Knox was a severe, strict man, but he wanted nothing for himself; all his life and all his work was for his Church and for Scotland. Henry VIII, however, thought only of his own good: the Church and the English people existed only for his own benefit and his own convenience. He was a foul-tempered bully who cared only for himself.

King Henry VIII was, like everybody else at that time, a Roman Catholic and was not interested in change. When he heard of Luther he called him a madman, and when a few people in England began to preach against Rome, Henry had them burnt at the stake. But Henry VIII was married to a Spanish princess, Catherine of Aragon, who had borne him a daughter, Mary. The time came when Henry no longer loved his wife and wanted to divorce her and marry a lady called Anne Boleyn. But the Catholic Church does not allow divorce. King Henry thought the Pope in Rome would make an exception for him, but he was mistaken. The Pope refused to allow Henry to divorce his wife.

Henry had sent an old English cardinal to Rome to plead with the Pope. When the old man came back with the news the Pope had refused, the king went into a towering rage. The poor old cardinal was sent to prison, but died on the way. Then Henry declared: 'If the Pope and his Church will not divorce me from my wife, I will have a Church that has nothing to do with Rome.'

The English Parliament had no liking for Rome or the Pope, and so at the wish of King Henry VIII a law was passed that, in

England, the head of the Church was no longer the Pope, but the king. Priests, monks and bishops who would not take an oath to recognise the king as head of the Church were executed.

So the Church that Henry had founded was not a new, reformed Church, like John Knox's or Calvin's or Luther's. It was the old Church, only now Henry and not the Pope was the head of it. In this way the Church of England is different from all the other Churches that came out of the Reformation.

The new Church, the Church of England, had of course to obey King Henry VIII. He divorced his wife, the Spanish princess, and married Anne Boleyn. She bore him a daughter, Elizabeth, who was to become one of the great queens of history.

But Anne Boleyn herself was not Henry's wife for long. He got tired of her, and did not even bother to divorce her; Anne was executed. After her Henry VIII had four more wives, one after another – who either died naturally or were executed or divorced.

Henry VIII was a cruel, brutal man, but strangely enough, the people of England liked him. They were glad to be rid of an Italian pope. They would rather have an Englishman as head of the Church, even if he was a selfish man. They liked King Henry VIII because he took all the land and wealth away from the monasteries and closed them down. They had come to think of the monks as useless, lazy men, who were good for nothing.

The common people liked King 'Hal', and when war broke out between Scotland and England, the English soldiers fought so well for Henry that the Scots suffered terrible defeats at Flodden Field and Solway Moss.

After Henry's death, England went through a hard time. His only living son, Edward VI, ruled only a few years before dying. The next ruler was Mary, the daughter of Catherine of Aragon whom Henry had divorced. Mary wanted to bring the Roman Catholic faith back, and the English men or women who spoke out against this were burned at the stake. In five years of Mary's rule three hundred people were burned for this crime. When she died, many people in England rejoiced and looked forward to the new queen, Elizabeth I, the daughter of Anne Boleyn, for she was a Protestant.

31. Mary, Queen of Scots

The new age, the new spirit, showed itself more among the common people than among the noblemen and kings. Columbus, Leonardo, Copernicus, Luther, John Knox, were all common people.

It was also the common people who welcomed the Reformation – at least most of them. The noblemen were more or less evenly divided for or against the Reformation. The kings were, to begin with, all against the Reformation.

The German emperor declared Luther an outlaw. The king of France solved the problem of the French Protestants by a terrible massacre. In one night, St Bartholomew's Night, thirty thousand Protestants were slaughtered in France. In Scotland, King James V tried to destroy the Protestant movement by executions and burnings, but the movement only grew stronger and in the end, the Church of Scotland was established against the will of King James.

In England, Henry VIII was also against the Reformation and heretics were burnt at the stake. It was only later, and for his own selfish reasons, that he established a Church separate from Rome.

But throughout all of this, England was more fortunate than other countries. In England, the ruler and the great majority of the people belonged to the same Church, the Church of England. When Elizabeth became queen, she too was in the fortunate position to belong to the Church that most of the people wanted: the Protestant Church of England. There were only a few Catholic sympathisers left in England.

Scotland was not so fortunate. For the most part the people belonged to the Church of Scotland, but the royal family, the Stuarts, remained Roman Catholics, and so did quite a number of noblemen. In Scotland, royalty and the people were divided by belonging to different Churches. That was the tragedy in the life of Mary, the daughter of James V.

When James V died, Mary was still a young child and she was crowned queen of Scotland as a baby. Her mother, a French princess, acted as Mary's regent (ruling until Mary was old enough). She sent Mary to France to be brought up at the Roman Catholic French court, and so Mary grew up in a religion and in a country quite different from Scotland and the Church of Scotland.

When Mary was only sixteen years old she was married to the young king of France, and became queen of both Scotland and France. It was the happiest time of her life. Mary was merry and charming, and the French courtiers were witty and amusing, they flattered and praised her. Her life was full of dancing, parties and games.

But this joyful time of Mary's life lasted only two years. First, her young husband died, and then her mother in Scotland died and Mary was called back to become Queen of Scots.

For Mary it was a heart-breaking change, being taken from her merry life at the court of France to Scotland, where John Knox and his followers looked upon merriment as a sin. Mary was a Roman Catholic and remained one, attending Roman Catholic services in her chapel in Holyrood Palace. The people of Scotland never quite trusted her, fearing she would try to bring back the Catholic faith. John Knox, who was by then an old man, said very unkind things about Mary in his sermons.

Mary, with her Roman Catholic religion and her love for fine, colourful dresses, for parties, dancing and games, was like a stranger in Scotland, even though she was the queen. Then she did something that made her less popular: she married a Catholic Scottish nobleman, Lord Darnley. The Scottish people did not like that at all. Darnley was an ill-tempered and coarse man, without education or manners. Mary was soon very unhappy with her husband, who probably did not really love her and had only married her in the hope of being crowned king of Scotland one day.

Although Lord Darnley did not really care for Mary, he was madly jealous of any man with whom Mary was friendly. She did not have many friends, but there was one, an Italian musician. He used to play for Mary and so gave the young, lonely queen some pleasure. But this enraged Lord Darnley and one day when Riccio, the Italian musician, was playing for the queen, Lord Darnley and some of his friends dragged Riccio away and stabbed him to death.

Mary never forgave Darnley for this murder, but she did not show how she felt. Soon another man was often seen in her company, a Scottish nobleman, James Hepburn, the fourth earl of Bothwell. Mary's husband, Darnley, was not very pleased with this friendship either, but now he kept away from Mary and hardly ever came to see her in Holyrood Palace. Then Lord Darnley fell ill. To everybody's surprise Mary showed great concern for her husband. She went to Glasgow and persuaded Darnley to be brought to Edinburgh where she could visit him daily.

Mary came regularly to visit the sick man, but one evening she came and apologised that she could not stay very long as there was a great dance at Holyrood Palace. That night, while the windows of Holyrood Palace were bright with the light of hundreds of candles, while colourfully dressed courtiers and ladies thronged the large rooms of the palace, while the sound of music and laughter could be heard, there suddenly came the roar of an explosion. The house where Darnley was lying on his sickbed had been blown up, and he and a page were found strangled in a garden nearby.

We shall never know who was behind the death of Darnley, but the Scottish people blamed Mary and her friend, the earl of Bothwell. When Mary married Bothwell three months after Darnley's death, it was too much. A great number of Protestant noblemen rose in rebellion against Mary. She was taken prisoner and kept imprisoned in a castle on an island in the middle of Loch Leven. She never saw her new husband again. He escaped to Denmark and later died there.

For a year Mary was imprisoned in that castle, but then a page stole the keys of the castle and with his help she escaped in a small rowing boat. Catholic noblemen now came to her aid, gathering an army to fight against the Protestants who had imprisoned Mary. Scotland was torn by a war between its own people, but in the end the Protestants were stronger. The Roman Catholics were defeated and Mary had to flee. No place in Scotland was safe for her. She fled to England, hoping that Elizabeth, who was a cousin of hers, would give her shelter and protection.

But Elizabeth gave Mary only a very cold welcome. There were still a number of Catholics in England who might well have tried a rebellion to make Mary the queen of England. Elizabeth was not going to take any risks. Mary was imprisoned in a series of English castles for nineteen years.

But even as a prisoner, Mary was a danger to Elizabeth. The English Catholics made plans to free Mary. All these plots failed, but they showed that as long as Mary was alive, the English Catholics were thinking of rebellion against Elizabeth. When, after nineteen years, another such plot was discovered, the English Parliament persuaded Elizabeth that Mary had to die, and so the English queen signed Mary's death warrant.

The queen of Scotland was led to a great hall in Fotheringhay Castle that was hung with black. Her servants cried bitterly, but Mary comforted them and said that for her, death was a release from prison. Calmly and proudly she walked to the execution-er's block in the middle of the hall and put her head down on the block for the executioner's axe. When the axe came down, it ended a sad life that had not known much happiness.

32. Elizabeth I and the Great Armada

Mary, Queen of Scots, was a warm-hearted woman of strong feelings. She followed her heart more than her head. Elizabeth, queen of England and Ireland, on the other hand did not have the warmth and charm of her cousin Mary. She did not follow her feelings, but thought over and weighed up everything she did. For a queen, this was the better way by far. Elizabeth, cool and level-headed as she was, had a great sense of responsibility: what she did was for the benefit of England. Mary, brought up in France, had little sense of responsibility for Scotland.

That is why Mary is one of the tragic queens of history, while Elizabeth became one of the great queens of history: she never forgot that she had a duty towards her people.

England was experiencing terrible dangers and hardships at that time, and these dangers and hardships mainly came from Spain. Spain at that time was immensely powerful. Enormous riches had come to it from the colonies in America and vast numbers of Spanish ships sailed the seas. The Spanish ships were larger and the number of ships greater than that of any other navy. The ruler of this mighty Spanish Empire was Philip II, the son of Emperor Charles V, who had declared Luther an outlaw.

Philip II was a devout Roman Catholic whose sole aim in life was to destroy the Reformation and to force the authority of the Pope back on the people who had broken away from Rome. He could do nothing about Germany, which was ruled by a brother of Charles V, but Belgium and Holland were under Philip's rule and in these unhappy countries the Protestants were burned by the hundreds. Philip's great ambition was to bring these 'blessings' to the people of England and, by force and terror, make England a

Roman Catholic country again. Philip nearly had the opportunity to do this, for as a young prince he married England's catholic Queen Mary, the daughter of King Henry VIII, who had ruled England before Elizabeth. But when Mary died, Elizabeth became queen. Now Philip made another attempt to get England under his power the easy way. Through the Spanish ambassador in London he sent a proposal of marriage to Elizabeth.

Of course, in his plan Elizabeth would have to become Roman Catholic, and of course, the English Protestants would be forced by terror and by persecution to return to the Church of Rome. But imagine what a mighty empire this union of Spain and England would have been. For an ambitious person – and Elizabeth was ambitious – it must have been a very tempting offer to become queen of England, Spain and the vast colonies in America. Elizabeth knew, however, that by marrying Philip she would bring terrible misery and suffering to all the Protestants in England, to the majority of her people. She refused the offer.

Philip was furious that his proposal of marriage had been rejected, but he soon had more reason to be annoyed by England. At this time the people of England began to realise that the future of their country was to become a seagoing power.

The ships of Prince Henry the Navigator had made Portugal rich, and the caravels of Columbus had given Spain untold wealth and power. Britain, an island surrounded by the sea, could only become great and prosperous with English ships and English sailors. It was at the time of Elizabeth that the English navy began to grow and the English sailors set out on the high seas.

These English captains and sailors were rather like the Spanish Conquistadors: their main interest was gold and treasure. They did not care how they gained their fortunes, as long as they could get rich.

The simplest way to gain wealth was by pouncing on the Spanish ships carrying gold and silver from America to Spain. The English sailors were simply pirates, but they were the most daring pirates in the world. One or two English ships would not only capture much bigger Spanish ships, but they would also sometimes attack one of the big Spanish ports in America, plundering it and sailing away loaded with booty.

King Philip of Spain was thoroughly annoyed with this English impudence. As long as Mary, Queen of Scots lived, Philip had hoped that the Roman Catholics in England would set her free, making her queen of England and Ireland. But when Mary was executed, there was an end to these hopes.

So Philip decided on one bold stroke that would finish off Queen Elizabeth, who had insulted him by refusing marriage, the English navy, which continued to rob his treasure ships, and the Protestant Church of England, which he had always wanted to destroy.

All three things should be accomplished with one mighty blow by the ships of Spain. Preparations began in Spain to send the largest fleet the world had ever seen against England. The fleet would not only attack English ports, but also carry a vast army to invade England and to occupy it. The dockyards of Spain worked in frantic haste to build more and more ships, and the Spanish warships from all over the world were called back to join the great fleet.

While all this preparation was going on, an English captain, Francis Drake, suddenly appeared with a handful of English ships in the Spanish port of Cadiz, and before the Spaniards recovered from their surprise, ten great Spanish galleons and twenty smaller vessels were sunk. As Drake sailed away, he caught a Spanish treasure ship and took from it a cargo of gold worth many millions in today's money. When Francis Drake arrived back in England, he said: 'I have singed the beard of the king of Spain.'

This important stroke made Philip II only more eager to punish England and, in May 1588, his fleet was ready. It was called the Great Armada. The Great Armada was a fleet of seventy large and sixty smaller ships. The large galleons of about five hundred tons were floating fortresses, carrying about three hundred men each. The whole Armada of a hundred and thirty ships carried twenty thousand soldiers and eight thousand sailors. Against this mighty fleet the English only had thirty-four much smaller vessels and fifteen thousand sailors. The English fleet was commanded by Lord Howard of Effingham, an experienced sailor, while the Armada was under the duke of

Medina Sidonia, who belonged to a very noble family and who knew very little about ships or sailing.

The English were certainly not afraid of the enemy's might. Francis Drake, who was one of the captains under Lord Howard, was at Plymouth playing a game of bowls when the news came that the Armada was approaching England. 'Time enough to finish this game and to beat the Spaniards,' said Drake. And he calmly finished the game before sailing against the enemy.

When the Armada appeared, beacon fires blazed from one end of England to the other to warn the people. Queen Elizabeth went to her fleet to speak to the sailors and her words stirred the hearts of the men.

As the Spanish ships came into the English Channel a strong gale blew up which made most of the twenty thousand soldiers so seasick that they were no use at all. Moreover, the high galleons could hardly be steered in heavy weather and the little English ships darted in and out between them, doing great damage and getting away before the Spaniards could hit back. This game lasted a whole week, during which time the gale grew fiercer and fiercer. More and more Spanish ships ran aground, and then the Spanish admiral made the mistake of ordering his ships to seek shelter on the French coast at Calais. The Spanish ships were all crowded together so the English sent fire-ships among them. These were ships filled with gunpowder and other combustibles that were deliberately set on fire and steered towards the enemy's fleet. The Spanish galleons, trying to get out of the way of the fire-ships, ran into each other.

By the end of the week the gale became so wild that even the English ships took to their ports. The Armada tried to get away by sailing around Scotland, but the roaring storm shattered so many ships on the rocks and islands that, in the end, only fifty vessels, broken and battered, reached Spain. The English had lost only two hundred men and not a single ship.

All over England bells rang and bonfires were lit. Elizabeth ordered that a special medal be struck in memory of this great occasion. On that medal was the inscription: 'God blew and they were scattered by His breath.'

33. Elizabethan Times, Shakespeare and Raleigh

When the Great Armada came, the people of England rallied around their queen. If the Spaniards had landed they would have found every Englishman and woman, from the peasant in their hut to the lord in his manor, ready to fight to their last breath. They loved their queen. When it became known she would pass through a street, people gathered together hours before and gave her rousing cheers when she came. They called her Good Queen Bess, but the courtiers invented better-sounding names for her. They called her the 'Virgin Queen' because she never married, and 'Gloriana', meaning the glorious one.

These were flattering names, and Queen Elizabeth liked to be flattered. With her auburn hair and delicate complexion she had a striking appearance, and she helped this striking appearance by wearing the most glorious clothes. She set fashions that made the clothes of wealthy women and men in England more colourful, more showy than they have ever been, either before or after.

Wealthy women's dresses were made of silk, or from cloth of silver or gold. They wore immense skirts that were made to stand out by means of petticoats with wooden hoops. Men's clothes were just as colourful: graceful jackets slashed to show brightly coloured linings; short, stuffed trousers; long stockings. Both men and women wore wide ruffs round their necks that stood out above the shoulders and high behind the head. Jewellery was worn by men and women, and many men wore an earring, a large single pearl or jewel.

The crude eating habits of earlier times disappeared, and for the first time people began to use forks, knives and spoons instead of their fingers. Houses, too, changed. With the invention of gunpowder there was no point in building castles that were like fortresses with moats and keeps. Now noblemen built graceful houses with large windows, wide doorways and spacious gardens. Some of these stately homes can still be seen today.

English ships sailing the seas brought trade, money and prosperity. Rich people could find more time for leisure and art.

One can say that at the time of Elizabeth, the Renaissance came to England. It did not show itself so much in paintings or sculptures, but in a different art: in poetry and in plays.

As the Italian people had become interested in paintings, so the English became fascinated by the writing and the production of plays. Queen Elizabeth had special plays performed for her at her royal court. Thousands of plays were written and performed in her time. The greatest of all the writers of that time, and arguably the greatest of all English writers of all times, was William Shakespeare.

At that time actors formed little groups, and at about the time of the Armada, William Shakespeare joined such a troupe of players in London. At first he was only a kind of stagehand. There is even a story that he used to look after the horses of people who came to see the plays. Then he became an actor himself and, after a time, he began to write plays for his group of players, who performed at the Globe Theatre in London. Shakespeare had learned the art of acting from scratch. He knew from his own experience what works effectively on the stage, and this no doubt contributed to his plays having the power they have to this day.

As the Renaissance produced Leonardo and Michelangelo in Italy, in England it produced the great genius of Shakespeare. But the Renaissance, the time of Queen Elizabeth, produced all kinds of colourful personalities with many amazing gifts. Such a person of many gifts who lived at that time was Sir Walter Raleigh.

The best way to be in Queen Elizabeth's favour was to flatter her. One day she was travelling in a coach through the streets of

London with some of her courtiers. As usual, crowds gathered to cheer her and, in order to show herself to her people, Elizabeth ordered the coach to stop, and stepped out of it. And there, right in front of her, was a big puddle of mud. If she made another step her dainty shoes would sink into the mud and her satin skirt would be splattered. As she hesitated, not knowing what to do, a young man stepped forward, he wore a fine scarlet cloak on his shoulders. In a moment he tore the cloak from his shoulders and threw it over the puddle. The queen could now step safely on the cloak and reach dry ground. She turned to the young man and ordered him to come with her to the court. He had spoiled his fine coat, but he had made his fortune.

The young man was Walter Raleigh, and he became the queen's favourite courtier. He had been poor, but the queen gave him large gifts of money and land, and later knighted him. But Sir Walter Raleigh was not only an elegant courtier, he was also a clever man and the queen followed his advice in matters of government. And so it came to pass that Sir Walter Raleigh changed the course of history. He once spoke to Queen Elizabeth and said: 'Spain has become rich and powerful through its colonies in the New World, in America. If England is to become a great nation, then we too must have colonies in America. We are not strong enough to take the Spanish colonies in South America, but Spain has not touched North America. Let us establish English colonies in North America, and we shall in time be greater than the Spaniards.'

Queen Elizabeth agreed with Raleigh's advice, but, even though he longed for adventure, she would not let him leave the court. Sir Walter Raleigh was not allowed to sail across the Atlantic to found an English colony in America, but he was rich enough to buy ships and to send men there. The first English colony in North America was established through Sir Walter Raleigh, and in order to flatter the Virgin Queen Elizabeth, this first English colony was called Virginia. It is now part of the United States and still bears the name Virginia.

As with the Spanish Conquistadors, the English colonists arrived in North America to find indigenous people already living there. The colonists fought with the local tribes, who were of course simply defending their homeland. But the colonists also learned from these Indigenous Americans. They learned from them the use of a peculiar American plant: tobacco. Soon the habit of smoking spread to Europe and made the colonists rich. Virginia tobacco is still grown today. Sir Walter Raleigh was one of the first to try the new habit of smoking. A servant who saw smoke coming from Raleigh's nose and mouth thought his master was on fire and threw a bucket of water over him.

Much more important was another American plant: the potato. In earlier times, when the wheat harvest happened to be bad in England, there was famine and starvation. Now people could fall back on potatoes when there was not enough bread. Raleigh was the first to have potatoes planted on his farms in England and so brought back something worth more than gold.

When Queen Elizabeth died, she appointed James VI of Scotland, the son of Mary, Queen of Scots, as her successor to the throne of England and Ireland. James VI had made no move to rescue his mother when she was condemned to death: he did not want to rouse the anger of Elizabeth and so lose his chance to become king of England and Ireland. At Elizabeth's death he then became king of Scotland, England and Ireland. For the first time in history the three countries were united and remained so.

Under King James, Sir Walter Raleigh could at last follow his thirst for adventure. As there was no gold in North America, Sir Walter Raleigh went to South America in search of a fabulous land called Eldorado where, so people said, even houses were made of solid gold. Raleigh and his men went through terrible hardships and dangers in the jungle, but never found Eldorado. When Raleigh returned to England, the Spaniards complained that he had attacked Spanish colonists and broken the peace between Spain and England. King James, who wanted peace with Spain, had Raleigh arrested and imprisoned. While Raleigh was in prison he wrote a book, a history of the world from the beginning to his own time. He was a very learned man as well as a wise statesman and fearless explorer. But King James had no liking for the man who had been the favourite of Elizabeth and, in the end, Raleigh was condemned to death and beheaded for having attacked Spaniards.

34. Francis Drake

The Age of Discovery, the Renaissance, the Reformation, are all names for the same period of time. When Columbus travelled to America in 1492, Leonardo da Vinci was in his forties and Martin Luther was a boy of nine: they were all children of the same new age, and in different ways they showed the same adventurous spirit. Copernicus, who surprised the world by saying that the earth moves around the sun, was twenty years old when Columbus discovered America.

An imaginary person who lived from 1500 to 1600 could have met all the famous people of that one century: Magellan and Pizarro, Calvin in Geneva, John Knox in Scotland and Savonarola in Florence, Michelangelo in Rome and William Shakespeare in London. They could have seen the Great Armada as well as Sir Walter Raleigh's first English colonists sailing to Virginia in America. This imaginary person would have met bold and adventurous spirits in all these people – for that was what they all had in common.

One of the English sea captains, in his own rough and tough way, had the same spirit of boldness and adventure that belongs to that time. Francis Drake was, at first, simply a merchant sailor, a sea captain who used his ships for trade. Nowadays we know that his trade was despicable, but in those days it was regarded by Europeans as ordinary business. He sailed his ships to Africa, where he and his men kidnapped African people and then shipped them to the Spanish colonies in America. The Spanish colonists paid well for these people, who they forced to work for them as slaves, and Drake was quite content in selling slaves to the Spaniards. This was many years before the Armada.

One day, with five ships under his command, Drake had sold a cargo of Africans to Spanish colonists, and had bought all kinds of goods in America that he expected to sell profitably in England. He was a skilled businessman. But on the way back, Drake's ships ran into a storm and took shelter in an island off the South American coast. This island was also a Spanish colony. The Spaniards seemed quite friendly and Drake had no reason to fear any harm from them. But when the gale was over and Drake's ships were about to sail away, the Spanish opened fire and three of Drake's ships were sunk with all men aboard. Drake escaped with two of his ships, but he swore he would make the Spaniards pay for their treachery.

At the time, England was at peace with Spain, and Queen Elizabeth was not at all anxious to start a war with Spain for the sake of three ships, so Drake began a one-man war of his own.

Drake prepared himself well for this war. For a whole year he sailed up and down the coast of America on which the Spanish colonies were until he knew every little bay and island. This American coastline, with its rich, great ports, was called the Spanish Main. He also made friends with runaway slaves. There were a few thousand people who had run away from their cruel Spanish masters and who lived in the jungle along the South American coast where the Spaniards could never catch them. These desperate gangs became staunch allies of Francis Drake.

Then he was ready to begin his own private war. His new allies had told him that there was a regular train of five hundred mules carrying silver from the mines of Peru to a sea port near Panama. From there ships carried the silver to Spain. Drake decided to take the silver before it got to the port.

He had two ships, which he left on a wild stretch of coast. Then he set out with fifty men into the jungle to ambush the silver-laden mules. Now Drake had been told that every twenty mules had one leading mule, and if this leading mule would lie down the other twenty would do the same. They had been trained to do so. When the mule-train came, the Spanish escorts were met with a hail of bullets and they ran for their lives without first counting the attackers. As soon as the Spanish soldiers were gone, Drake and his men made the leading mule lie down and all the others did the same. Drake and his men now took the silver off the mules. They buried one part in the forest and returned a few months later to get it. But they took as much as they could carry to the ships and sailed away.

After this first blow, Drake gave the Spaniards no peace. Up and down the Spanish Main he sailed. He stopped any Spanish ship, and his men went aboard and took away any valuable cargo before the Spanish ship could sail on. Drake's ships were soon loaded with plunder. When he had looted two hundred Spanish ships he returned to England where he was welcomed as a hero.

The next time Drake set out, it was with the help and approval of Queen Elizabeth. That voyage became famous as the voyage of the *Golden Hind*. It was the first English voyage around the world.

At first, Drake had no intention of sailing around the world. He had already plundered the Spanish colonies on the east coast of America and now he wanted to attack the fabulously rich colonies on the west coast. To do this, Drake had to sail through the Strait of Magellan.

Drake set out with three ships, but two were lost in a storm and only one ship, his *Golden Hind*, made the voyage. The *Golden Hind* sailed through the Strait of Magellan and appeared on the west coast where nobody expected to see an English ship.

So Drake and his men simply sailed into the harbour in the city of Valparaiso, shot up the Spanish ships lying at anchor, and then seized the whole city and took what they wanted. They sailed away and, on the way out, captured a Spanish galleon carrying a fortune in gold and jewels.

By now the enraged Spaniards had got a whole fleet together and were waiting at the Strait of Magellan to catch Drake on his way back. But Drake got to know about it and decided he need not go back through the Strait of Magellan: the world was round and he could go back round the world as Magellan's ship had done.

So, like Magellan, he sailed across the Pacific Ocean, past India, around Africa and reached England after three years absence, and with the greatest treasure ever gained by a single ship. Most of that went to Queen Elizabeth, but he was knighted by her and became Sir Francis Drake. The *Golden Hind* is one of the famous ships of history, like the *Santa Maria*.

The next time Drake sailed out, he performed the boldest stroke of his life. The capital of the Spanish colonies was Cartagena, an immensely rich city with strong fortifications and great guns pointing towards the sea. Drake let his ships feign an attack from the sea, but in the night he led a thousand men through swamps to the rear of Cartagena. The defenders were completely taken by surprise, and in a few hours, Drake was master of the city. The citizens of Cartagena had to pay him an enormous ransom before he left and sailed back to England.

Although no enemy ever got the better of Sir Francis Drake, he died of malaria while sailing on another venture against the Spanish Main. He was one of the most renowned seafarers in history.

Index

Floris
Books

For news on all our **latest books,**
and to receive **exclusive discounts,**
join our mailing list at:

florisbooks.co.uk

Plus subscribers get a FREE book
with every online order!

We will never pass your details to anyone else.